My Lighted Path

The Spiritual Journey of a Boston Black Woman on A Road Less Traveled

Thelma G. Cromwell-Moss

Table of Contents

Preface

I write these memoirs with the prayer that a dream will be fulfilled to allow me to do my research and establish a manufacturing firm in AAG Industries, Inc. (An Act of God Industries, Inc.)

The Fellowship of friends and scholars who have assisted me and critiqued this book have clarified for me what should remain or be removed from the text. I will define my experiences in a positive manner, positively plus and positively minus, because no matter how difficult, everything happens for a reason and is ultimately for good.

I have kept journals and written through-out my life. I am presently past three-score in age. I believe that my poems, songs and writings are memories that chronicle my journey to the Creator God or to the One Source of the Universe. At this point in my life I believe in the teachings of Moses, Muhammad, Buddha and Jesus which probably makes me Jewish, Muslim, Buddhist and Christian. I have come to the parting of ways with organized religion and now appreciate the messages and teachings of the Anointed Ones all over the world. There are probably many more Anointed Ones such as Lao Tzu, Mary Baker Eddy or Sukunishisama whose addition to the Sacred Volumes of the World might be under appreciated. However, I know that whatever Divine Spirit allows that is *'sweet on my tongue and warms my heart'*, is good for me.

I know we are more than the sum of our physical parts. I know that I am a Spiritual being having a physical experience. My journey, which is taking place within the small bubble that I call my world, has left me with the satisfaction that *'I can do all things through the Creator God who strengthens me within the stillness and silence.'*

At the same time, this is not a religious book but a story of my life experiences. I believe that I have enjoyed a unique life. This book is a series of incidents that people who have similar experiences can relate to at various points along the way. We are becoming aware and intent on making a difference.

Dedication

I dedicate these memoirs to my Gram'ma 'Liza; my mother, Amatullah Sabreen Shakir (Archie bell McCarter[McCotter] Cromwell,) (AHCHI – her Native American name given by her mother); my children Willie James Moss, Jr., Marwan Jonathan Moss and Namala Thelma Moss as well as my grandchildren, starting with Khalil Marwan Moss, who was christened on the day of his birth, Satori Malik Shakir, (Whose name means...The Enlightened King serving God). To my brothers, Abdul Kareem Shakir, born Anthony Leo Cromwell, and George Walter Cromwell, Sr, John Cromwell, Robert Cromwell and sister, Vivian Cromwell, I can only hope that this remembrance brings them no pain, hurt or embarrassment. These pages may be read by my children and few others. So be it. I just want them to know something about the life I've lived.

I lived the first half of my life being obedient, timid and afraid. I have since learned fear benefits no one. There is nothing God-like about fear. The second half of my life can be lived freely in thoughts knowing that I can go directly to the Universal Source of Light and Love and none could prevent me but myself. I hope you and all readers accept this idea of freedom before you leave this physical side of life.

To the many that were parts of my learning, those that inflicted pain, distrust, emotional, physical and verbal abuse, thank you. Your efforts reminded me to depend on the Creator and "let God"; also, those who supported me with a kind word, a smile, financial help and a belief that I had the strength to recover and move forward, thank you. Your efforts reminded me that I was not forgotten and the Creator was still in charge. The prayers that supported me have carried me on the wings of love. I confess my ignorance of the many pains that I may have caused others, those acts were not intentional and I ask the Universal Source and you for forgiveness.

I am grateful for having grown. I grew from being a physical fearful child to a quantum mind-consciousness learner, questioner, seeker, challenger and light-filled soul. I have coined a phrase relating to what I have become. I am a MUTT, a Multi-ethnic; Ultimate; Thinking; Threat. May the second half of my life be a reflection of what I have learned. That is, may I be an agent of harmony and love which brings a change and benefit to the energy of the planet.

By Divine permission it is my intent to publish my memoirs, complete the dream that will not only create employment, enhance education but also leave a footprint on the path of humankind.

Today

It is 2012. I am editing my book, reviewing the pages that tell the story of my life. What to include. It has been a fantastic journey. In seventy years I've been privileged to meet liars, cheaters, racists, deceivers and manipulators who perceive that they are 'getting over' for one contrived reason or another. They think no one sees. God sees. The sad part is they lose in spirit, which is the most important place one should not lose. "What does it profit a man if he gains the whole world and loses his soul?' I pray for them.

I have also met persons of all religious and non-religious persuasions striving to be of service to God and humanity by serving humans, animals and all life on earth; being examples of their belief. I pray with them that we can divert the prediction of total destruction by changing the energy of the planet, through prayers, offering Universal Light and being change agents by example, in our spiritual patterns.

Quo Vadis? What is Phase Two? We need to research and solve the problem of malaria, clean water, and diseases. I'm going to be a part of that if allowed by Divine Arrangement. We will manufacture and offer employment.

I know this will take money from deep pockets. I believe it will come. Ideas and dreams from the Universe are not meant to be fostered and die. It will come from those visionaries of all nationalities who see and understand that it is TIME. Make no mistake; the CHANGE will come with us as LEADERS or FOLLOWERS.

Chapter I – My Childhood

My earliest memories

I remember the sweet smell of a grayish-blue bedspread with circles or what I would now call "fleur de lis." I saw the curtains flowing in the breeze as if reaching out to touch me. I remember being on my back and smiling at the curtains. There was something peaceful about that time. I can also remember rolling off the bed and hitting the floor and crying. I later learned that my brothers would sit on the edge of the bed causing a slant and I would roll off, they thought that was funny. When I was older, one of them said, "How do you think you got so much sense, we dropped you on your head."

My mother grew up in New Bern. Her story is at fourteen she was raped. My cousin tells the story differently. She says that my mother and father fell in love when she was fourteen and he was sixteen. In Gram'ma 'Liza's house there was an upstairs and downstairs. On the first floor was a couch used as a bed for company. My mother conceived my brother on that couch. At that time in her life she had considered becoming a nun. She told me she had her bags packed. It never happened. She never cried out, if she was being raped, because Gram'ma Liza would have come running from upstairs with a shotgun. So either story being couched in embarrassment or in the emotional state of love, the effect was that my grandmother never again had a day bed in her living room. My brother was born. The rest is history. Both my brothers were born in New Bern, I was born in Boston.

In Boston, my mother and father always had parties on weekends. My dad played left-handed guitar and would sit in with visiting notable bands at the Hi-Hat and other clubs on Columbus and Massachusetts Avenue. After their sessions, they came to our house, also known as Tony and Bell's place. There they would find fried chicken, hot rolls, potato salad, greens and macaroni and cheese. There was always food, drinks and card games. My mother played the piano and sang. My dad didn't drink and he was the best Whist player until the day he died. No 'kitty whist' games for him, you played the cards dealt, straight bid whist. My room was the first room next to the front door and I would try to leave the door open so I could see everyone come in wearing fancy clothes and laughing and talking. Those evenings always seemed like happy times.

My Dad

My father was a disciplinarian who believed in using a razor strap, ironing cord, wooden drum stick or a slap upside the head to correct behavior. That was how he had learned and he could only pass on what he knew. That was the way it was in those days. Unfortunately, my brothers were the recipients of this harsh treatment. When they came home with school work, my father was the person who would hit them upside the head if they didn't have the correct answer quickly. I watched, and maybe out of fear or maybe because I was sitting at the table when they did their lessons, I learned

2

everything that they were learning. So, I learned and I was smart. In that day no one talked about dyslexia, you were slow or dumb. I used to sit in my room and cry when my father beat my brothers. He didn't just put the fear of God in them, but with a razor strap he instilled fear. With what I know now, I wish it had never happened.

In the South we had been taught to say "yes, ma'am" and "yes, sir" to adults, white and black. In Boston that was considered a hold over from slavery and in school we were constantly reprimanded for using those terms. We were only to say "yes' and "no.' When we went to school my brothers were chased home with stones and bricks because they had a southern accent. There were always fights. One day my oldest brother came home with a bloody nose, crying. Tired of this everyday hassle, my father sent him back outside and warned him that if he didn't beat that boy, he was going to beat my brother. Needless to say my brother whipped the tar out of him, and the bricks and fights stopped. We were then accepted.

We had rules to live by. No elbows on the table. Children forget. The chair is too low and putting your elbows on the table gave you leverage to handle your knife and fork. As quickly as I put my elbows up, I was hit with the back of a knife right on my funny bone. I learned, no elbows on the table.

My father was also playful and full of fun. He would put on the radio show of the *"the Shadow"* or some other scary radio mystery and hide in the closet sending out weird sounds and ghostly music. Then just as my brothers and I were about to run out of the house, he would jump out of the closet and we would all laugh and sigh and hug each other.

Finally we got to know the routine and we would sit through three and four hours of stories on the radio while he moaned and clanged in the closet. He could hardly breathe in there. He got tired of that game after a while.

My father received harsh discipline, and gave that treatment to his children. He came up in an era where discipline was offered 'to beat the devil out of you.' I can understand why there are laws against beating children, but I can draw the line between spanking and beating. I guess that was my Christian upbringing of 'spare the rod and spoil the child.' I've learned many different methods of discipline. I've used the age old sequence consequence rule. There is nothing that exists or happens for which there is not a consequence. Think about it. Inhale, exhale; don't breathe; smile, don't smile; everything has a consequence. Learning how to make good choices early is important. I know that you must have the child's attention, so that the child becomes aware of <u>their</u> significance, responsibility and obligation to choose. Never to be fearful of choosing, but to learn from poor choices and then choose wisely. If you don't learn to choose, others will choose for you. Hopefully you are an example of good choices. If not, teach the lessons of your poor choices. It is never too early to train or teach. However, first, I know that you must have the child's attention. How to secure that? The options are many.

Granny

My father's mother, Granny, (Laura Suggs) was a cook. She always made mouth watering rolls on Sunday and I would sit and watch her. She never gave out her recipes. She was a Canadian from Nova Scotia and a gambler. They tell the story of the time that she had a winning hand in poker and would not leave the table even when her water broke. As a result my dad was born in a cab. My mother had been given a letter that my Granny had written to a friend saying that she was bringing this colored girl up from the South to help her out in her rooming house. The only problem with that was that my mother and father were married and he had two children by her. Granny never accepted the fact that my dad had chosen 'that southern colored girl' for a wife.

One time Granny, did not buy my oldest brother a Christmas gift. My mother felt that he was being ignored because he was too dark. So my mother, with the three of us in tow, not so politely took all Granny's gifts back and threw them on the porch. "You buy gifts for all of them or you buy for none.'"

I grew up in Boston in a black and white world where neither side talked about the content of your character only the color of your skin. How light skinned you were, how straight your hair was, what color your eyes were. My Uncle Harold had blue eyes. Many of my cousins could pass for white and did. There was always something I didn't understand. My cousin had married a dark-skinned man of Cape Verdean descent. Granny loved him. If you were Cape Verdean and black as the ace of spades, you were okay. But if you were dark-skinned from the south you were not. Go figure.

Color was an issue in my family growing up. It was a sign of the times. This is the climate I lived in.

Uncle Norman

I remember Uncle Norman Cromwell. He seemed tall as a mountain to a two year old. He was my fathers' uncle from Canada, living in Cambridge or Boston. I loved him. He always had candy or something for me when he came. One evening when I was two years old, I remember being in a red velvet dress, wearing the ruffled panties that Gram'ma Liza had made for me. Every one was playing cards. I went to my dad and asked him for a penny, and he said no. So as not to be penniless, I went to my uncle Norman, climbed on his knee and asked him for a penny. "Sure,'" he said, and he started to reach in his pocket to give me a coin. Suddenly I felt my self being picked up from his lap and then I knew that I had done something terribly wrong. My father spanked me. I was crushed. I cried more because my father was angry with me than because of the three pops I got on my behind. He had never spanked me before. I will never forget his words. "Don't you ever ask any man for money. If I can't give it to you then you don't have it. Do you hear me?'" Yes, I heard. He had never before spanked me and never been angry with me. That was a lesson for me because at five years old my mother and father were divorced. I honestly believed that since he couldn't give me (money) then I was obligated to make it for myself. I didn't feel worthy to accept money from men. It was a harsh lesson in my life, to always work hard and provide for myself. This has benefited me because whenever the road was rough, finances low, I was all alone and depression raised its' ugly head, I knew I was responsible for the next step with Divine Guidance. I had to move on.

Parent Relationships

When my mom and dad fought, it was like cats and dogs. All our pots and pans had dents. They used to hit each other over the head or body when the arguments reached a fevered pitch. I thought they all came with dents until my mother bought new pots when I was six years old. When I was four years old Gram'ma 'Liza came to Boston. I will never forget that time because she was a seamstress. She took an old brown paper bag, pressed it out on the table, made a pattern, did some cutting, and hand sewed me more underpants with ruffles. She showed me how she designed things. They looked and felt just like store bought. That was my Gram'ma Liza. She told my mother she would never come to her house as long as my mother lived with a man that beat her. She never did as long as my mother and father were together.

My parents worked, he worked nights and she worked days. Dad had a pool hall on Sarsfield Street. He would take me with him while he cleaned up the place and shot pool. There was this lady who would always stop by to chat. Daddy would sit me on the pool table while they would talk. When I was five, my mother and father got a divorce. The lady who used to come by the pool hall became my father's next wife. I had to pass by the building that they lived in on the way to school and her children would scream out the window, "We got your dad." I cried and found other ways to go to school so I would not have to pass their house.

The Promise and Guardians

After the divorce Gram'ma 'Liza came to visit in Boston. I told her how my own father with his new wife had once walked across to the other side of the street, rather than speak to me. I told her I hated him. As tears rolled down my cheeks, I said that I wished he were dead. She dried my tears, held my face, looked me in the eye, and said, "One day he will need you. You will have to feed him, give him money, and maybe even take care of him.'" I said, "He'll die before I'll ever feed him or help him.'" She looked at me sadly, "It will happen and when it does promise me you will feed him and take care of him.'" She made me promise. I also remember she looked into my eyes and said, "You're an old soul.'" There was no explanation. I remember her face looking at me as though she saw within and beyond me with a knowing smile. I felt spellbound. I remember because just then my dog, Tuffy came running into the kitchen wagging her tail and jumping on me, it broke the spell. I went out to play with my dog. It's interesting how and what you can remember.

I lived in the same city with my father and had no contact with him until much later in his life. To this day, I still have the Samsonite luggage that he gave me on my day of graduation from high school. The only gift from him I ever received. After years of no contact and no acknowledgment from my father, my father reentered my life.

One day my husband, who had joined the Prince Hall Masons, called me from the kitchen. He said that he had brought a brother of the lodge to visit. Wiping my apron I came to the door only to see my father. I didn't know what to do and neither did he. He just said hello. I said Hi, and went on back into the kitchen. Later I asked my husband, why he had brought him here. He said that he wanted the children to know their grandfather and maybe I could let bygones be bygones. All the pain that welled up inside of me at that time, caused me to walk out of the room and go have a good cry. Here was the man who had hurt me, my father, being friends with the man who was beating me.

When I got a divorce my father came to the house. We talked. Then he put his arms around me and we both cried for a long time. We bonded. He helped me with the children, getting them to school, picking them up. I paid him, because he liked to play the numbers or scratch tickets; he wasn't working and gas cost money.

I had no friends but Divine Spirit sent me protectors. There was this community person named Cleophus Clark. He lived around the corner. He worked with children in the community. I had to be six or seven at the time, and I would go to his apartment and he always had two or more kids like me needing a place to 'hang.' He always had something to teach. I learned from him how to carve soap figures, paint them and protect them with nail polish. It was a program that forced me to focus, be patient and accomplish something. Many times in haste I cut off a foot or broke a piece of the soap and had to start all over or make something else. He taught me to basket weave and how to make chains and things with colored gimp. He kept me busy. His home was my haven after school while my mother was out or still working. He kept me off the street. He was the angel sent to make the times when I was lonely and sad, become alive with new knowledge and training. Later he moved to Rhode Island and I never saw him again. I'd heard when he died. I will always remember him.

Eight Year Old Experiences

When I was eight there were many life changing events.

I started my menses. My mother felt she was unable to talk to me about sex or female development, so she sent me to see Dr. Price. Dr. Price was the only black physician in Boston who served the black community. We talked and he gave me books to read. On my way out the door he asked me what I planned to do when I grew up. My quick response was, "Save my people.'" He looked surprised and said, "'That is not your job." I just smiled.

I always felt that I was here to make things better, serve the community, build a better world and make a difference. That was and is still in my spirit but I have learned late in life that by improving myself I am improving the world. Being an example of God Consciousness and letting one's light shine are really all that the Creator God is asking of each human being.

I am required to Do No Harm! I cannot change people, they must change themselves. Like myself, they must pack all their mental and spiritual luggage, in their body which is their personal car, and take their personal journey on highways or roads. It's their choice, and the consequences are theirs, as well.

At eight years old, I was a latch key kid, with the key hung around my neck. One day I was turning the corner of my street and this white man, who was well dressed, asked me if he could use my bathroom. He said he really had to go and didn't want to go in the street because that was vulgar. That made sense. He asked me how was school. We were talking, and then he asked me if my mother was home. By that time my mother and father were divorced. A bell went off in my head. I was told not to talk to strangers and certainly not bring people into the house when my mother wasn't home. I was in trouble. He looked at the key hanging around my neck. I said, "no." He seemed to be pleased with the answer. I lived at 23 Walpole Street on the third floor. There were two apartments on each floor with a landing. You went through the outside door and then another door before you started up the stairs to the apartments. I got to the outside front door. I said, "'No, my mother is at work." A broader smile came on his face. "But, my daddy's at home. He works nights so I'm never home alone." His face started to crease, and my heart was pounding. We walked up the steps to the second door leading to the stairs that would take me to my apartment.

I started walking faster and also started calling, "'Daddy, I'm home and we've got company." I turned around to see him, and I smiled. He had stopped following me. "Oh, its, okay'," I said. "'Come on up, I know that Daddy is getting up." Then I started up the steps again a little faster. He didn't move. By now I was sweating and scared to death. Because hadn't my mother and father told me not to talk to strangers. So, I called up again. "'Daddy, we got company, wake up." By now I was at the second landing and running up the stairs. I looked back and he was running down the stairs and out the door. No one had to ever again warn me about talking to strangers. From then on, I kept my key inside my clothes and never looked up when called by a stranger.

Thank you, Angels and Spiritual Guides for protecting me from my youth and ignorance.

I was eight in the third grade. Given my mother's "rape,'" she was always cautioning me "Do not let boys touch you. It is wrong.'" I took it literally. What did I know in the third grade? When we went to recess there was a line that separated the girls' playground from the boys'. This one boy (last name Gold) would always run over from the boys' side and tap me on the shoulder, hit me, or push me. I was paranoid from my mother's warning that if a "boy touched me it was wrong." As I look back, it was probably considered a childhood infatuation, puppy love. But at that time in my life "he was touching me and it was wrong.'" I kept telling him not to touch me, to stop. So one day, I came to school with a knife. This time when he ran to the girls' side and pushed or touched me, I turned around and slit his wrist. The blood squirted all over the place. I was in shock. "Well,'" I reasoned, "he'll never touch me again.'" They rushed him to the hospital. They said that I had cut a major artery, and I was going to jail if he died. They called my mother from work. I was released in her care and told to stay from school a few days. Well, he didn't die. My mother's statement to the teachers was, "I guess he won't touch my daughter again.'"

I was traumatized. I was sure he was going to die. I went home that night and prayed for forgiveness, and I asked to see God. As I lay in my bed, a golden light appeared at the foot of my bed. It got larger. I put my head under the covers but the light shone through the comforter just as though the comforter was not there. I thought I was crazy. The ball of light grew larger. I started getting scared and full of fear. In my head I heard "Are you afraid? Do you fear?" I answered, yes. Just as quick as the light started, it vanished, and the room was totally dark except for the moonlight coming in the window. I have never forgotten that incident of light. I promised God that I would never kill anyone. I've since re-evaluated that phrase to exclude protecting myself if my personal life were threatened. Hopefully force with equal force.

Dear Holy Spirit, counsel, guide and continue to protect me. I am a stranger moving on this less traveled road.

Chapter II – Family

Living with a single mother

After having gone through my parent's divorce when I was five and facing all the ensuing years where my self-esteem was destroyed, I was sure I was going to hell. I was sure that there was something evil in me that God had to clean out. Hadn't the church told me that I was a sinner and now that I had stabbed someone, it was clear that if I didn't straighten up, I would never see God. I became religious. I became a good Catholic, no meat on Friday, weekly confessions and catechism classes to atone for hurting another human being. I believe my religious awareness began when I realized there were Douay and King James Versions of the Bible. Until then I thought that all Bibles were the same. I took pictures with Bishop, later-to-be Cardinal Cushing. I sang in the choir and as a soloist. I was ready to change my evil ways.

One time after catechism class, Sister Eugenia told me I had to stay until 3:30 p.m. because there was something she had to do with me. I told her that my mother wanted me home by 3:00 p.m. The class would make me late getting home. Her response was that, "she was closer to God than my mother, so I had to obey her." I got hollered at when I got home late. When I told my mother what Sister Eugenia had said, she put on her coat and marched me right back to the church. She asked for Sister Eugenia and informed her, "'I had this child, she does what I say. If you want to tell a child what to do, have your own damn child."

That was the last time I was at St. Richards Church. St. Cyprian's Episcopal Church was at the corner of my street, so I started to go there. It was similar to a Catholic church except there were no nuns and the priests married. Darnley Corbin was the music director and so my brothers and I sang in the choir and participated in the life of that church. The predominance of the church members was from the West Indies. Some of the notable children coming from that era were Sylvan Campbell, who later became a doctor and Louis Walcott who later became Louis X, my brother George Cromwell, a singer, "the Dapper." He wrote the song, *The Funky Chicken,* and *'Washed up.'*

Most children aspired and became role models of citizens because of the no nonsense moral backgrounds of the church and family. I once heard one of the mothers talking, and she explained that she was 'beating' her teenage son. The noise was so loud from the boy that the neighbors called the police. When the police officer came, she informed him that she beat him so that the policeman, looking at his 'bully club,' would not have to beat him. The policeman left. We were more afraid of our parents than we were of the police.

Another incident happened to me in the third grade. Ms Melia, my teacher, told the class that if any of our mothers beats us, we could tell her and Ms Melia would have that mother put in jail. Finally, I smiled. That was music to my ears. Since the divorce, I was always getting slapped or spanked for something. Most times I didn't know what I had done. Armed with this new information, I came home to inform my mother that she could not beat me any more. Ms. Melia, my teacher, would have her put in jail. Fury came and settled on that reddish-black face. She looked me dead in the eye and informed me, "I brought you in and I'll take you out.'" There was no doubt in my mind that she meant it.

The next day, my mother escorted me to school. She confronted Ms. Melia in the classroom. "Are you the teacher that told my daughter I better not whip her?'" I looked at Ms. Melia, my savior, and I saw all the blood draining from her face. In a weak voice, she started to say yes, but never got it out. My mother with hand on hip informed her that she would "whip her ass." I had never seen this side of my mother in public. She had left all her diplomacy and civility at home. I looked at the teacher who was going to save me from this crazy lady who whipped me for cause and no cause. Then my mother looked at her and pointed her finger and said "'And you can call the cops, and I'll whip his ass too." My mom, the fear of God and country went through me.

This woman, my mom, was not afraid of either this teacher or the cops. She was not playing. Gone was my door to freedom from this woman. My mother went on to inform this teacher that I was being sent to school to get an education not home training or moral values. She was doing that at home as well as providing food, clothing, and shelter. The only thing Ms. Melia said was, "Yes, Mrs. Cromwell.'" That was it. I was bewildered.

Yesterday this white woman was going to put my mother in jail if I reported her and today she was a puppy. I thought, my teacher, my savior was going to take me out of this crazy woman's house and restrain her, but instead my mother put the fear of God in both Ms. Melia and me. From then on, you can believe when my mother's messages had conflict with any outsider, mother's message was the law.

My mother was devastated by her divorce. She truly loved my father. After the divorce, she and my father used me as a football between their pains. She would look at me and say, "You look just like your father, don't you think you're so cute." She would send me to the Masonic Hall on the corner of Sarsfield and Tremont Street to get a nickel. I couldn't come home until I got that nickel. When I got to the Masonic hall, they would call my father out of his meeting because his daughter was there. I would ask him for a nickel. He would holler at me by saying, "'What's wrong with you, do you think I'm made of money." I would cry and he would tell me to sit in the corner until he finished his session. I was humiliated. I sat for hours, usually until dark because I couldn't go home or my mother would beat me for not having the nickel.

Through the ages of five to nine, I was very shy. The anger between my parents was directed at me. I was the last child, born nine years after my oldest brother. I was a mistake. My mother never let me forget that she tried to abort me by falling on the train tracks, lifting heavy pianos and anything else that she could do. My mother never missed a chance, in private, to tell me that she really never wanted me. In public when people would tell her what a good girl I was, she would say thank you, so kindly. But when no one was around, she had a litany of stories of what she did to abort me. She described how she fell, stomach first, on the trolley tracks hoping to get rid of me. Her final response after this iteration was "'But God must have brought you here for some reason, cause you're still here."

I loved my mother, but throughout my life I didn't like how she treated me. I felt she catered to my brothers all her life but with me, privately it was a constant battle. I reminded her of my father, and that was not good. Maybe some of it was my growing into an adult female and her fear of what I might become. But mostly, I believe, it was because she loved my dad and I looked so much like him. So, if I were to say that I grew up in a dysfunctional family, it would be an understatement.

Mama Dear and Aunt Margaret

I spent a lot of time with a woman I called Aunt Margaret and her mother, Mama Dear. Yes, Tyler Perry, we even had Mama Dear's (Ma Dear) in the North. When I was six to nine years old, Aunt Margaret was my "'other'" mother. She took me to several churches including, Tremont Temple, Park Street Church and her church home, Christ Temple in Roxbury. It was there that I became disenchanted with the Christian religion. Reverend Fisher and Lemuel Hunter, the choral director spent much time training me to mesmerize crowds with music and speech. I thought it false because I could start moaning at the right time or sing on cue and those sisters would become so emotional that they would give up their money to the church leaving themselves wanting. It left a bad taste in my mouth even though I sang in his yearly pageant for Easter weekend, where, as the character of Jesus he died and rose on Easter Sunday. People came from miles around to see this man (who looked like Jesus) rise on Easter.

We ate at Mama Dear's on Sunday's after church. She had several foster children. We had to wash our hands and present them to her before we could sit down to eat. We would stand behind our chairs until everyone was present. The boys were taught to pull out the girls' chairs, and we would all sit down to bless the table. Mama Dear would bless the table with the food on it, and then began the difficult part. We would sit there inhaling the smells of meat, hot rolls, greens, and mashed potatoes. She was a great cook but she had her ways.

You could not eat unless you could recite a Bible verse. If you did not know one, she had a long box on the table that had verses in it and you had to pull one of the cards out and memorize the verse right then. Depending on which side of the table went first, someone said, "Jesus wept" or "Moses slept." The rest of us got stuck sitting there memorizing verses so we could eat. So you can imagine we rushed to wash our hands and sit next to Mama Dear. It was a challenge to sit smelling that good food and spend time on memorization.

Aunt Margaret took me to Tremont Temple and Park Street Church. I sang at Park Street Church. I sang with a young white boy evangelist. The next thing I knew they were petitioning my mother to let me go with them to Africa. Of course, my mother's response was a definite, no.

Introduction to the Nation of Islam- age nine to eleven

During the ages of nine and eleven I experienced much training. I grew and changed. By the time I went to the Hyde-Everett Middle School, I had very low self esteem. A high school student had to walk me to school because girls use to beat me up and take my money or hit me, "just because." I was fearful of everything. In that day children were tracked in school. I overheard the principal, Miss Sullivan, talking to my teacher in the fifth grade that if they could make me a good secretary then they would have been successful. So I was guided to the commercial course and not allowed to take the exam for Latin school because I wasn't considered to be "very bright."

I became aware of the Nation of Islam when I was ten years old, in 1949. My mother had been concerned about me meeting people and having friends because I stayed to myself a lot and read the Bible and other religious writings. One day she said that she had met a great group of people at this lady's house and that I should go and meet them. "They talk about the Bible and you might have something in common."

At that point in my life I had studied the Bible, many other religious and spiritual tenets and I felt pretty knowledgeable about the subject of religion. So I went over to meet someone I was later to call Sister Middie and her son Brother Joseph X. I listened to their discussion of the Bible and started asking questions. Finally I asked a question they could not answer. Aha, they're not so smart, I thought. 'Ah well, we don't know the answer, but we can surely have someone here who can give you the answer. Brother Malcolm X. Several times I went to their home meetings where this Malcolm X was supposed to show up and never did. I figured he was scared. Since I had beat up their purveyors of "truth," and this mystery man, Malcolm X, was a no show, I guessed that he just wasn't willing to tackle me.

Finally, they said that this Minister Malcolm X was coming to town and would be at this building on Columbus Avenue. He would be willing to answer all my questions.

I arrived at the Temple of Islam on Columbus Avenue in my white straw hat with a blue ribbon hanging down the back, white gloves, white socks and white patent leather shoes, quite the epitome of Christian garb of the day. I was searched and ushered into the front row and awaited this Malcolm X. From the time he set foot on the podium pounding the history of the black man and the slave master, I was numb. I had been trained by Christian clerics on how to use the podium and music to bring the masses into a state of mind to pray and give up their money, but I had never heard a man talk about the life experiences of people of the world with such conviction. These were experiences that I shared and knew first hand.

He talked about being a convict and how Islam had changed him. I was spellbound. At ten years old anyone would be. He finally ended his presentation and asked if there were any questions. I was the lamb being led to the slaughter. He had been primed for me. I asked my question, and before I knew it, he and I were bantering back and forth. Of course I was not prepared for him. With my stomach wrenching, I sat down. When it was all over, I shook his hand and promised myself that I would read more and study and catch him the next time. So I did just that, no ex-convict was going to out-talk me or out maneuver me on the Bible. Not in this life. So I read more, and each time I would take what he said and go study more and come back and challenge him again. It got to be a surety that if I was there and Malcolm was there, we would be having an interchange.

One day I was in the audience when he asked if water was a food. No one answered. By then I no longer had to sit in the front row. In my place farther back, I stood up and said, "If you want to get technical," and a voice behind me said, "'Oh God, now here she goes getting technical." I started to sit down when a voice bellowed from the podium," "'don't you sit down ,sister, if you want to get technical do so. Tell me what you have to say." "Well, Minister Malcolm, if we believe that anything that nourishes the body is a food, then water is a food because it has minerals and nutrients that do indeed nourish the body." "Thank you, sister. That makes sense. Now listen to me don't you ever sit down when you know that you are right or you have an idea that has some value. Don't you listen to people trying to tear you down. You stand up. Do you hear me?" "Yes Sir" "Don't you ever let me hear of you not standing up stating the truth no matter to whom or what." "Yes sir." Teary eyed, I sat down.

By then I was going on eleven and wanted to join the Nation but my mother would not consent, so I had to wait until I was twelve. I wrote my letter and did my Shahad-dah when I turned twelve. Someone on earth had handed me the keys to education and freedom of thought. "You know,'" Malcolm would tell me "there are no dumb Muslims. A Muslim is the essence of knowledge, wisdom, and understanding. We are never the aggressors but we will protect ourselves when attacked. You must study and get good marks and be a credit to the Nation.'"

Influence of the Nation of Islam

At twelve years old I was in the ninth grade. My previous educational pursuits were not spectacular. I just got by. I seldom spoke. Islam breathed new life into my lungs and I came into Girls' High School a new person with an agenda, to be the best student any one had ever seen and make the Nation proud. Because of past low performance and expected incompetence, I was placed in the commercial course to become a secretary with office skills.

During my first few weeks in school, I had a bookkeeping class. I would sit at the back of the room. The teacher would make a list of numbers on the board and by the time she drew a line and asked us to add it up, I would holler out the answer. I thought it was cute. I enjoyed seeing her face turn red as she glared at me, knowing the answer was right. She would say, "'I didn't call on you Ms. Cromwell." I would nod my head. "'Boy, this being in high school was going to be a snap," I thought.

Finally, she had had enough of me and my wise cracking ways. Instead of turning red and glaring at me, she walked up to the desk with her ruler one day. I thought she was going to hit me. Instead she stared at me and said,'" Get out of my class." Then I knew I was in trouble. If my mother found out I had been acting up in class or if Malcolm learned I had been kicked out of class, I could never live with the embarrassment or disgrace. "'You get your books and things and leave this class." "'What did I do?" She certainly was not going to throw me out of school for having the right answers, or maybe that's how the whites keep us down. Everything was running through my mind at that time. "'You get out of here. Go to the office and tell them to put you in the college course and don't ever let me see you in this class again." I just stared. "'What?" "You heard me. Now get out!"

That's how I got into the college course. Now, I was really scared. Hadn't I been told that I would make a good secretary? I wasn't smart enough to take the Latin school entrance exams. That's just how those white folks are; they put you in a situation to see you fail. What was I going to do? Let me explain, the principal of the school, Mr. McInerney, was a former admiral in the navy. The head of the English Department was a female, and was a former major in the army and God only knows how many other military persons were running this all girls' public school. They were going to make sure I was unsuccessful. I just knew I was being primed for failure. Conspiracy, conspiracy, conspiracy.

Well, Malcolm said I must be the best so that's what I tried to be. Here goes. For someone who never spoke up through middle school, I became the spokesperson for everything. I took on every class with gusto. I met Mr. Long, my best teacher in high school. He was an accounting teacher but he also taught law, elocution and speech writing. I started having difficulty in my classes because I couldn't keep my mouth shut concerning the misleading information about the black experience in our text books. I was put out of history class and given independent study because I disagreed with some of the information and ideas in the books. I couldn't accept passages, indicating that we were found in trees like monkeys and brought to this country to be civilized, trained and educated. I would spend the weekend in the library and bring books to class to refute the text. The teachers did not appreciate any of this.

Dear Holy Spirit, thank you for my bookkeeping teacher, the head of the history department, and Mr. Long. My apologies; I don't remember their names. They made a lasting impression on me. I can still see their faces.

Finally, I was at the crossroads again, but this time my law and speech teacher, Mr. Long, told me, '"Thelma when you are right, don't back down. Stand your ground." I fell in love. This was not Malcolm, advising me, but a white man, in the system. He was educated and was guiding me to fight for what was right, champion the underdog, and hold to the truth. Following such words of advice has made my life more difficult than it might have been, as I journeyed down the road less traveled. But Spirit has guided me and I sleep in peace at night. I have learned to be grateful and accept the life I have.

Public Speaking and Tony Bennett

I won contest after contest in oration and speaking. I was the first black girl representing Girls High to win a state cup in oratory. I loved my four years of high school. They were spent in studies and working. I missed the girl years, though. I didn't make time to learn the nuances of boy-girl relationships. I would have had a better understanding in choosing a husband and partner had I had that experience. That I regret.

At age fifteen, I won a public speaking contest for the Red Feather, the precursor of the United Way. I was seated at the head table next to Tony Bennett. He had just released a hit song, "I Left My Heart in San Francisco'." I was so proud to be sitting next to him. I called him Mr. Martin throughout the luncheon. We talked and talked and I kept calling him Mr. Martin. I had to be polite, that was my home training. Then the moderator said, "Now we will have Tony sing his new hit record, Ladies and gentlemen, Mr. Tony Bennett.' He looked at me with a smile and got up and sang. And Ohhhhh-hhhhh, the humiliation. I wanted to disappear, melt into the floor. I had called him Mr. Martin all during lunch, and he never once corrected me. I will never forget his graciousness. He came back to the table and shook my hand and smiled. I knew that he had forgiven me for my ignorance and my youth.

I observed graciousness and humbleness and I thank you dear Holy Spirit for allowing Tony Bennett to cross my path.

Learning experiences in organizing

Was I a rebel with a cause? Maybe. After all, I was out to do the right thing and impact the world. For example at age fourteen, I was working in the kitchens of Beth Israel

Hospital while in high school making fifty cents an hour. There were five to six students from Girls' High School working as kitchen aids. I worked after school and on weekends. My mother said she needed the money for us to live, along with the support of my father. I tried to organize the students to ask for twenty-five cents more, seventy-five cents in all. We met and agreed to ask for more money. One way or another, our boss who was the head of Nutrition, found out about it. We all agreed to go down together and ask for a raise. Everyone was with me.

We walked to the door of her office. I opened the door and said, "'We would like to talk to you about a raise." "We, who? She said." I turned around and no one but me was in the doorway. Undaunted, I asked for a raise. I made the case that I needed more money, and that I was coming in at 5:30 a.m. and doing the work of the full-time workers, etc. She informed me that no raise was possible. I thanked her for her time and quit. I left and went down the street to Woolworth Five and Dime Store and got seventy-five cents an hour.

I learned something about organizing and standing up for your rights, or better still, I learned that when and if you should make a stand, know your enemies, know your supporters, know yourself, and make sure you are clear about what you are willing to live with, and your bottom line. I wasn't willing to continue to do the same work as the full-time people, and accept less pay. Looking back, I had no place to go. My mother was depending on my money to make ends meet. It was a dumb move. Maybe.

God looks out for babies and fools and I was certainly one or the other. Once again, Divine Spirit was guiding, protecting and moving me through crises.

Experiences with my mother and leaving home.

My mother never remarried. She loved my father. She told me that she hoped I would not make the same mistake she had made. "I want you to remarry."' She had a few good opportunities to remarry but she never did.

One time a man came to the door with a dozen long stem roses. I had never seen a man giving a woman long stem roses except in the movies. I just knew that my mother was going to marry him. She didn't. When I asked her why, she said, "The next man I marry will say, "thank you", when I hand him a cup of coffee." This man had come to the house and seen our furniture and suggested that, with her furniture he would get a house and they could get married. Her vision was that she had bought this furniture with her first husband and didn't want to take this furniture into a new marriage. She wanted new furniture and a new home. He thought she was crazy, and the man with the roses never returned.

I dreaded the times she went to court so she could get what he "owed' her. I remember the social worker coming to our apartment in Mission Hill. I told him that I was tired of having to go through this monthly crisis. He informed me that my mother had a right to expect my father to take care of me, his child. I told him that I would get a job and take care of myself. I was fourteen years old and got a job at Beth Israel

Hospital. I gave her my check and she gave me just enough money to get back and forth to school and work.

My mother never had a childhood, since she had become pregnant at fourteen, which gave her no time to grow up and enjoy life. When my brothers left home, she was stuck with me. I loved her, but she wanted to have a life. She would have her male friends at the house. I couldn't blame her for that. But many times, the door was locked and chained. I had to wait outside in the cold until she opened the door. As I was coming along, I think there was resentment or maybe it was fear that I might end up like she had.

I'm not sure. I know it did not help to have a daughter believing that fornication was a sin. Muslims could not do it, why should Christians? That was the dichotomy for anyone living with me at the time. Every thing was black or white. Many times I would look at her and she seemed so sad. I always felt I was the cause of her pain.

I came home one afternoon. My mother was ironing in the kitchen, and an FBI man was sitting on the couch and wanted to question me. I informed him that he could meet me at the Temple, and I would answer any questions he might have there. I guess my mother felt this 'Moslem stuff' was getting out of control. I was getting out of control, especially with me confronting the FBI. By this time I had been in the Nation of Islam two years. We were having disagreements about how much time I was spending at the Temple. I refused to eat pork. "'If I buy it, you'll eat it," she said.

When I was fourteen years old, I left home. I remember she picked up a broom to hit me, because I refused to cook or eat pork, I told her I would kill her if she ever hit me again. She believed I meant it, and at the time I believed I did.

My family was involved in music as far back as I could remember. So it was not unusual that we attended the South End Music School from the time we could read. My brothers played piano and drums. I sang and played the piano. Most of the children of St. Cyprians Church attended that music school. By the time I was thirteen, the school had closed and I started taking lessons at the Academy of Music owned by Ms. Anna Bobbitt Gardner on Claremont Park in the South End. When I left home at fourteen years old, I went to live with Ms. Anna Bobbitt Gardner. She was my piano teacher. I taught beginners how to read music and studied voice there as well. I was given a Marian Anderson Scholarship through her school to the New England Conservatory. Because I was a Muslim, I asked Malcolm X, who was my friend and mentor now, if I could take it. I will never forget his answer. We met on the corner of Massachusetts and Columbus Avenues and he looked at me sorrowfully and said, "Sister, I asked the Messenger, and he said no sister should be on the stage. I'm sorry." Much to my dismay, I refused the scholarship, but I promised God, if he would allow me to maintain my voice, that one day I would sing.

When I left home, I had not consulted Malcolm. He was greatly concerned and he worried about my move. My mother was constantly calling me to come back home, and I was refusing. He would always talk in parables or analogies. "You know sister, two queens can't sit on a throne. You being out here on your own is not the best thing." Of course, I assured him that I was making the right decision. He continued to counsel me, suggesting that I return home and learn to live in my mother's house. My mother and I talked. She agreed not to cook my food or feed me pork. I went back home. Incidentally, twenty years later, as a Muslim, my mother made Hajj. Only the Creator God, as Allah could manifest this one.

Thank you, Holy Spirit for bringing Malcolm into my life and for your guidance through him. His words have been a constant reminder to live an honorable life.

Chapter III – College, Change and Islam

Boston University and College life in 1956

I graduated from high school at the age of sixteen with a partial scholarship to Boston University. I wanted to be an engineer. On my first day in architecture class, the instructor came to me and said that he did not teach women and that I needed to find another career choice. At that time there was only one other black person in the class, and he was male, so I transferred to education and business. My new classmates were Korean Veterans. I was sixteen years old. A counselor suggested that I hold off and wait a year before taking my scholarship. What I heard is," 'We don't want you here'" and of course my mother informed them that they had given me this scholarship and I was there to stay. They were right. I was inexperienced but I guess I was meant to be there because I introduced the school populace to "Black Muslims." The sad part for me is that most of these black students and veterans had traveled around the world, spoke several languages, and were pretty much the elite of the black community. I was a kid from the projects. I am sure they saw me as a crazy nut caught up with those crazy "Black Muslim" people. Maybe.

I believe Boston University was the first college where Malcolm spoke. I had him scheduled to speak at the school of Divinity in 1957. To this day when I meet some of the ministers who were at that meeting, they tell me they were influenced to bring about community awareness by the speech of Brother Malcolm. That was not bad for a novice, I think. At the same time, Martin (Dr. Martin Luther King, Jr.) was at Boston University. He and I talked several times and I tried to persuade him to come to Malcolm's lecture. In that day and during that time, "Muslims and especially so-called Black Muslims were not accepted by the majority or by the black community, and Dr. King would have nothing to do with "those people.'" That meeting didn't happen. It is interesting how, years later, a meeting of two champions would be played out on the world stage by the coming together of Martin and Malcolm with their love of service to the black, poor and the international community.

I was always searching. Looking back, I find it interesting how my thinking gradually changed and what I learned from the resident Minister of Boston University, Dean Howard Thurman, and the lessons of agape love. He was someone I always enjoyed talking with at that time. I would explain the teachings of the Honorable Elijah Muhammad and he would always talk about agape love. I found him engaging but figured he would wake up one day and agree with me. He was someone I admired and respected. Just in case he's listening, I want him to know that I finally understand agape love. *You were right, the love of the Creator God wins.*

Boston University and Growth in the Nation of Islam

I left school for several reasons mostly because a minister said, "You women going to college and taking the seat of a black man, get out and give a black man a chance.'" When I left school, rest assured, no black man took my seat.

I got a job at an insurance company. My Muslim clothes became a factor, and I was terminated because my clothes were a health hazard. I appealed and won the case. My work was not the problem. The company let its bias show when they realized I was not foreign born but an American Negro, a Black Muslim. That was in 1958-59.

From that time until 1962 when I married, I began to understand much about this Islam that I had accepted and the interpretation that I was being given. There was a teaching from the rostrum usually influenced by the speakers' experience, a training being given usually influenced by the understanding of the teachers or leaders, and a law or rule coming from Chicago and 'the Messenger.' I was ignorant of this Islam, not stupid. I questioned and challenged what I did not understand. I looked for guidance in local leadership. It soon was apparent that the leadership was struggling to understand Islam, as well.

Later, some people would call the Nation of Islam a social experiment. Others would call the recognized change in behavior and attitude of its' members 'a resurrection' of the down trodden ex-slave. That would not be my interpretation. For me, it was a time of preparation. Since I was very young and in school, constantly reading as much as I could, I 'got it' when Elijah Muhammad would challenge us and our behavior to live in a civilized society. No one wanted to live next door to drug addicts, murderers, thieves, prostitutes, cheaters and liars. In the South in my day, we could not play with their children. 'If you lay down with dogs, you're bound to come up with fleas. Birds of a feather stick together.' It was always around a moral compass.

If those people changed their behavior and 'cleaned themselves up' than they could be accepted in a civilized society. We could change, we must change and Islam and Qur'an would assist us. In desegregation we lost the experience of teaching our children, being role models; going to our stores and building an economic base and educational empowerment. I wanted us to be equal in everything and never lose our spiritual compass. It was clear to me then that the push for equality, the change from segregation to desegregation did not benefit all the children of Native Americans and ex-slaves. Some were and some were not. The community of blacks from the South to the North had changed and much of the cohesiveness, independence and our God consciousness were disassociated. Our need for self and community fulfillment, growth and independent development was being impacted leaving us dependent on welfare and government subsidies.

When I was growing up, it was a disgrace to be on welfare. Neighbors would offer help, food, and child care, whatever was needed to help you get back on your feet so you would not have to go on welfare. But when I needed that support, I was glad it was there. My personal thoughts and community had changed. I was required to participate in a multi-ethnic global community, Malcolm and Elijah Muhammad stressed that; Islam taught that.

From ten years old to age twenty-two, I was an active, participating student of the teachings of the Honorable Elijah Muhammad. I traveled in car caravans to New York, Chicago, Springfield, and Hartford. Wherever the Messenger was speaking and I could go, I went. Whenever Malcolm or Thomas J. was speaking, and I could get there, I was there. Minister Louis was now the Boston minister. They used to call me the "shadow'" or Ministers Louis, Malcolm and I, the three musketeers. They were my brothers and idols. Malcolm was my confidant, teacher, and friend.

Later Louis X (Minister Farrakhan) was my minister at Temple #11. I ran the University of Islam, became a lieutenant in the Muslim Girls' Training and General Civilization Class (MGT&GCC) and headed the education of women under his leadership.

I administered the University of Islam at Temple #11 under Minister Louis X. It was a regular school and we also taught and trained the children in Muslim prayers and culture. Minister Louis Farrakhan was my friend. He supported my growth and work in the Temple. As I look back now, I hope that my ignorance in education and teaching in no way impacted negatively on any of the children.

Divine Spirit was kind. I was walking through Franklin Park one morning and heard a cry out, "Sister Thelma, Sister Thelma.'" One of the young men stopped me to tell me that

I was the only teacher who ever taught him anything and he thanked me for being in his life. That made me feel good and I thanked the Creator that I had made a good impression in someone's life.

After being a lieutenant for a while, I felt I should be a captain. Here comes ego. At that time Arlene and I were lieutenants. I couldn't understand why I couldn't be a captain. Sister Clara pulled me aside and told me that I had to be married to become a Captain. How absurd! I knew as much, if not more than most of the married women. Here's ego again. Today, as I look back over my life, I believe with my experiences, I could now qualify for captain, colonel and maybe a one star general.

Again, I can apologize for my ignorance to any humans that I may have led astray because of my lack of understanding. I am also thankful that the Creator God never left my side.

At nineteen years old, I bought a two family house on 17-19 Fayston Street, Roxbury. At the time, the HUD manager informed me that I was the youngest home owner he had ever approved. My mother and I lived on the second floor and we rented out the first floor. Then I bought a new Peugeot. It came with a kit to repair it which was good because I was always traveling. I don't ever remember using it.

After work, I was always traveling, to Springfield, Mass and Hartford, Connecticut. I was enamored with the tall, black minister called Thomas J. X. Many times I went because Minister Malcolm was teaching. One evening after the teaching, Malcolm asked me if I wanted to go to New York. I was eighteen and elated. I thought that Thomas J was going as well. No, just Malcolm and I. No escort, no third party. I thought that it was strange because I had always been escorted, always with a third party. A single sister was never in a car alone with a single man. We talked from the time we left until we reached New York. We talked about marriage, raising sons, family, and then the bomb dropped. I looked at Malcolm, with no thought to the impact of my statement, "Oh, I would never marry a light skinned man." I was thinking of being married to a tall dark skinned minister in Springfield and having dark skinned children.

I saw the blood drain from his face. The laughter and discussion changed. He asked what I wanted from life. What did I know what to want? I had been told, guided and controlled. Malcolm was my brother, my confidant and my friend. We arrived at Temple #7 in Harlem. Captain Joseph opened the door and helped me out of the car. I heard him ask Malcolm, "Well, what did she say?" "I never asked her," was his reply. I believe rightly or wrongly that my fixation on color caused me problems. My life could have been different and history would have had a different ending. I will never know because it never came to pass. I believe, to this day, a marriage to Malcolm was not meant to be. A Spiritual, Divine arrangement had another destiny for him. I had much growing up to do, and my destiny was yet to be determined.

When Minister Thomas J. married, I was devastated, I cried. Malcolm called me, and I cried. What else could a naïve girl do but cry? I told him, "you don't know how it feels." He responded, "I know, I know." I continued to cry and we parted with the greeting of "Peace'" (As-Salaam-Alaikum). There are no accidents in the Universe and everything happens for a reason. I have come to believe that. We are allowed many opportunities and we make choices, and the consequences are there for every choice we make. My pain and whetstones of people, places, and things have tuned and polished me to a better place, by Divine arrangement. It is all good. I threw myself into my job, my responsibilities as lieutenant and the advancement of children and women in the Temple. I considered my life complete. I had traveled, had been the lead character in a play, nothing to do now but get married. I was only twenty. In those next few years I spent many hours in Chicago. We had been told to get permission but the Messenger had told me to come anytime. So I did.

My experiences with Elijah and Clara Muhammad

I believe I am one of the fortunate students because I was able to go to Chicago and eat at The Honorable Elijah Muhammad's table many times. I would meet and talk one on one with him and his wife. He and I would sit at a table pouring over passages in the Bible; I asked him questions. His life and example in spiritual and business development were setting a high standard for me. I remember at one dinner I saw okra on the plate. Instead of sending the plate back and asking that the okra be removed, I ate what I wanted and sent the plate back. He suggested that the next time there was something on my plate that I didn't eat to send it back to be removed. Someone else might eat it. "'We don't waste food." Just like my Gram'ma 'Liza. I began to understand the similarity and influence of his Southern background and mine and the simple moral code that he brought to his teaching.

One time I saw small girls playing in his yard, sitting on his door steps, not in Muslim garb. I was incensed. Who let these children wear polo shirts and pants, no head piece? I was appalled because in our temple it was unacceptable for females to go without their heads covered at any age. I spoke to Sister Clara Mohammad. I wanted to know who was responsible. "'I am," she replied. "They are children. Let them be children for as long as they can. They will be adults for the rest of their lives. They will decide if Islam for them." This was a contradiction from what I had been given to teach in the women's classes. This Islam was natural, peaceful, intelligent and felt so right. I guess by then I was not so sure that I was being a responsible lieutenant, because what she did and what I was being told were contradictory.

Another time I was at his table, seated across from a blue eyed Caucasian in Muslim garb. I informed him that I could kill "the so-called white devils." His face became sad and shocked. He raised his hand over his face and brought it down showing a quieter persona. His statement to me was that Muslims did not hate people because of their eye or skin color. What was he saying? Didn't he preach the destruction of the 'white devils.' I was puzzled. After several meetings with him, I came to realize that the anger, hate and pain that I had suffered at the hands of whites had to be let go and I had to work on me. I had to define my journey to Allah, the Creator God.

I started bringing my Bible to his house and would ask him questions. What does this mean? What does that mean? He told me that Russia and America who were enemies at the time would become good friends. I listened but didn't understand. He told me many things that have happened and others that will come to pass. One thing he told me, I Remember and pass on: 'A time will come when the earth will be filled with so many God-Conscious minded people that a negative thought will be crushed or removed and the world as we have known it will never happen again. Not an inkling of negativity in the mind consciousness of those living.' I might not live to see that day and you may not believe that day is coming but in Elijah's words, "just keep breathing."

I continued to ask questions. I was a lieutenant; I had concerns about brothers teaching women in the MGT classes. He told me, "Tell the men to stay out of MGT. I teach you and you teach the women." At one point he told me that many women would come to Islam. I questioned him, "'Dear Holy Apostle, do you think these women are going to wear these long dresses?" I expected him to say, "'wear them or don't come in." What he said was, "'Wear what you are willing to defend." In the 1950's, for me, that was a bombshell. All these regulations of form and fashion were not what God was looking for, God wanted your heart, your voice, your spirit turned towards him.

There was no compulsion in Islam. You lived, dressed and behaved according to your understanding. The closer you came to your God consciousness, the greater change inside and out would be reflected. Brother Elijah and Sister Clara Muhammad were the examples. I was never able to give this message to the women because the whole Boston atmosphere was changing and changed. Finally, the Messenger told me that I needed to read and understand Qur'an. He gave me two red volumes written by Muhammad Ali, the scholar. He told me to study them and get back to him for the remainder of the volumes. I was never able to carry out his wishes or return for the other volumes.

I learned from him, what my Gram'ma 'Liza had been teaching me as a child. The Spirit of the Omniscient gives the same message, to every nation, in every language throughout time, if we would only listen. I became an example of what I believed he had taught me. I was no longer the same Muslim I had started out to be. The social pain and experiences of the South were being released and I began to follow the tenets of the Qur'an. Malcolm was no longer in the Nation, neither was I. Those days were fraught with suspicion, guile, deception, and lies. By then every one was questioning everything. My Islam no longer existed.

I buckled down, that's what you do in a storm, and I rode it out. My mother who was by then a Muslim could not talk to me. I was the infidel. Those were some of the most heart wrenching years. A joyous life was turned into a quagmire of innuendoes and lies. At that point people were creating their own Islam, and I hunkered down to create a functional new life given my understanding.

"Sometimes I feel like a motherless child . . . a long way from home."

ORGENA

ORGENA

I was Sister Sylvia in the first production of *ORGENA* in the late 1950's. *Orgena* was a play that displayed the life and times of persons of color. It dealt with the enslavement, colonization, dehumanization of Native Americans and Africans becoming American through the slave trades. It showed the removal of their history. The play depicted the demoralization of the children of Native Americans and ex-slaves to alcohol, drugs, mental dysfunction, wife beating, religious idolatry, and self-debasement. The play tackled themes such as the belief of righteous Muslims prior to coming to America, the Native American, the wife beater, the prostitute, the Christian black preacher, and the historical behavior of white rulers on trial before a world court.

I played the part of the last prosecuting witness and explained the plight of the so-called American Negro. The play was a trial of the life, times and treatment in America of the Native American, slaves and children of ex-slaves. There was laughter, music, pain, and food for thought.

An interesting event after my performance at Carnegie Hall; an African Muslim presented me with a three carat diamond.. He had come to many performances and proposed to me after this one at Carnegie Hall. Captain Clarence informed me that American Muslims did not marry foreign born Muslims. I was told to return the ring and I did. That was that. I was about nineteen or twenty. My life was regulated and controlled and I accepted it because I believed that "my brothers'" were looking out for my best interest.

It would be difficult for many to believe that in that day a group of so-called "Black Muslims" could keep Islamic Laws to the point that men and women didn't shake hands. I've since learned of other situations happening at that time, criminal and thug behavior, but this was my life. The beauty of Islam is that there is honestly no compulsion. No matter what is done in its name. You wake up one day and realize that you go direct to the Divine. You are held accountable for your deeds.

In Qu'ran, I believe there is an 'ayah' (verse) explaining our standing before the Creator God on the Day of Judgment. You try to blame anyone and everyone for the decisions you have made so you don't have to reap the consequences. However, Iblis (Satan or the Deceiving One) says,"Blame me not, I only called you, you came." By Divine Permission, I still have choice. Only I am responsible to the Creator God for my decisions. I allowed my life to be controlled by others because I didn't know better. I acted as if the Divine Spirit did not live in me as well as every human. That thinking was an error. As I look back now, a little older and wiser, I am most appreciative of the protection offered me by my Muslim brothers. I was able to avoid the entrapments of youth in an urban environment and focus on my road to God Consciousness and higher goals. Sometimes that is a plus and sometimes a minus, depending on time and maturity.

The Color of Your Skin

My father, who had straight hair and was light to passing white, and my mother who had reddish-black skin like her mother, met in New Bern, North Carolina. I thought she was beautiful. She was given a Native American name Ahchi, misspelled as "Archie Bell" by the white census takers. His mother hated southerners and made no bones about it. However, she went South to marry a southern man named Suggs, who was to my knowledge, not of dark hue.

In the North my light skin was a ticket to do things and in the South, with my dark red skinned cousins, I was a disgrace. My cousin's didn't want to walk with me. My Gram'ma 'Liza found out how they were treating me and she whipped them. When we were out of her sight, I was made to walk behind them. They called me shit color. I would sit in the sun until I burned so that I could get dark like them. Their skin was dark red, and they had high cheek bones, from the Native American side of the family.

One day I saw Gram'ma 'Liza coming to me crying and she pulled me out of the sun. She told me I would never be her color or the color of my cousins. "God made you what you are, be proud of that."

Later in life I was talking to someone about my childhood. She informed me that I wasn't light skinned at all, she was considered Octoroon which I later learned was an offensive term for somebody who has one black great-grandparent and no other black ancestors. I grew up in a time when a 'drop' of black blood made you black. I am happy to live in a time where I see more and more 'content of character' being utilized as the unifying perception in time and place.

Regardless of my skin color, because of Islamic teachings at that time, I called myself Black. In Boston we were still dealing with the big N for Negro or Capital C for Colored. People identified themselves as West Indians, Islanders, American Indians, Portuguese, Cape Verdean and the anathema of all in Boston, Southerners.

By ten years of age, I had experienced most of the southern life style, first hand: the White or Colored toilets and drinking fountains, the back of the bus, and the cohesiveness of the black community, as we came together in crises and supported each other. This was my southern life and my true learning and training in a community of love.

Thank you, Dear Holy Spirit, without these experiences, I would not understand the extremes we humans can exceed, and the necessary STRONG INTENT and STRONG WILL we need to bring us back to our God Consciousness, our moral compass, and our spiritual core.

Chapter IV – Life in New Bern

My Life in the South and Gram'ma 'Liza

I remember at seven years old being put on a bus going to New Bern, North Carolina to see my Gram'ma Liza. Since no one could take me, my brother George was singing professionally and my other brother had gone in the army, I was entrusted to Travelers Aid. I remember a sweet, blond haired lady sat me in the front of the bus, pinned a button on me with my name and told me, "Don't you move from this seat. Your uncle and grandma are going to be looking for you when you get to New Bern. So don't you move.'" I was all decked out and happy to be grown enough to ride the bus alone. I had my meals in my bag and off I went on Greyhound.

We got to Maryland and the bus drivers changed. He told me to get in the back of the bus. I refused. I told him I couldn't leave this seat because the Travelers' Aid lady had put me here and my uncle and grandma would be looking for me here in the front seat of the bus. I would not move and he declared he would not move the bus unless I moved. Finally an older black man (Colored in that day) came to the front of the bus and took me by the hand. He said, "Honey you're in the South now. You come back here with me.'" I tried to explain to him that I couldn't move. "It's going to be alright.

We'll make sure you get to see your uncle and grandma.'" I walked to the back of the bus with tears in my eyes. I will never forget the harshness of that southern white bus driver nor the soft-spoken black man that assured me I would see my grandma and uncle in New Bern, and I did.

I loved going to New Bern. Every vacation and every summer I ended up in New Bern with My Gram'ma Liza. She was tall, they said she was five foot ten or five foot nine. She stood erect and stately. She never stooped over or lowered her head. She kept her shoulders straight and walked erect; she could throw a shoe across the room with the accuracy of a knife meant to get your attention. We had space, a garden of vegetables, chickens and more space. Everybody seemed to know everybody and we depended on each other because of segregation. I was happy. We got along. There were other families like mine with light-skinned children but we all got along and had fun.

There were side shows. A man would come by every other week on a flat bed wooden truck. He would tap dance, play the guitar or banjo and sing. After that another man would come out and sell 'ruematizim medicine,' "Hadacol.' Gram'ma 'Liza would always send me down with one dollar to buy her a bottle of "Hadacol.' I later came to believe it might have had laudanum or alcohol in it; but what ever it was, it eased her pain. I loved to go and watch the dancer perform and sing. Those were good times.

My Gram'ma washed and ironed "white folk's clothes.'" We washed them and hung them out on the line in freezing weather and in summer. Her fingers would knot and curl from arthritis but the Hadacol medicine would help. I was taught to iron the sheets and pillowcases without "cat faces."' If it was not right, she would wet it down, and I had to do it all over again, '"and this time do it right." I first learned how to iron with flat irons. You put them on the stove, heat them up, then run them over candle wax, and then touch the wax to see if it was just right, and then iron. You never burned a sheet or pillowcase. I was real glad when we got an electric iron, but it cost more to do the ironing. Then we folded the washed and ironed clothes, put them in a basket and took them to the back door of the 'white folks' house. She would give us the money agreed on, and I went home and gave it to my Gram'ma.

Working in the Tobacco Field

I remember one summer I wanted to go with my cousins to the tobacco farms to work. My Gram'ma 'Liza was against it. I pleaded, and the truck driver said he would look out for me. He dropped us off and waited around; I guess he knew I wouldn't last. I saw those big leaves and a tobacco worm. That was it. I wanted out. He drove me back to the city and home. I guess the city girl just couldn't hang. Later that evening when everyone came home from the fields, I was the laughing stock of the evening about how I was running from the field to the truck. I never again asked to go work in the cotton fields or the tobacco farms.

Southern Church Experiences

Of course I grew up in the church. I attended Catholic mass at 7:00 a.m. or late mass at 8:00 a.m. In the south the

Catholic church was partially desegregated. We all went to mass at the same time, in separate sections, but at the same time. At 10:00 am I went to the AME Zion church, Sunday school and then service. We were usually there until 1:00 p.m. That was the church that my grandmother went to. Between 1-3 pm we ate at a church or at home and by four it was Pentecostal and then an evening service.

No one worked in our house on Sunday. That was the Lord's day. No clothes washing or ironing, no dancing and no 'messin' around. Sunday church clothes never got worn on any other day. Killing chickens, picking your vegetables from the garden, everything was done on Saturday. We cooked most things on Saturday and warmed up things on Sunday. We were always on our porch before the sun went down. Sometimes there were no lights and you carried a flashlight to find your way. I always loved to listen and watch the church singing and the dancing. I watched a lot, which was fun.

I remember once going to a church in the evening where the drums and music were religious and rhythmic. My cousin and I came home talking about what a great band that was. Gram'ma 'Liza heard us and told us that was not what we should be going to the church for: Going to the church was to meet God and learn something religious. So she told us not to go to that church anymore. Did we listen? NO. I blame my cousin Edna, she was always getting in trouble and taking me with her.

As soon as Gram'ma 'Liza went to sleep one Sunday afternoon, we snuck down to the church and listened outside.

One of the members saw us and invited us in. Now Gram'ma couldn't blame us if the church people invited us in, could she. They put us on the front pew. Right up front. Of course, we started tapping our feet and clapping our hands and swaying in our seats from side to side. Then this lady in a white dress took me by the hand and led me to the altar. In my mind I was screaming, what's going on here. She and I knelt down and she started praying, holding me by the back of my neck, she told me I couldn't leave until I saw Jesus.

Now I knew I was in trouble. I had come to experience the music not get into a religious experience. She just kept praying and I was getting more and more frightened. Finally, I got up and hollered, "'I see him, I see Jesus," and ran down the aisle and out the door. My cousin had left and was running home. It was late and the lights had just come on. We were supposed to be home. We took a shortcut, jumped the fence, scratched our legs, tore our skirts and were sitting on the back stoop when Gram'ma 'Liza came to check on us. Never again, no, never again did we 'visit' that church.

Uncle Richard

We had a ritual in my Gram'ma's house, every body had to work. If you didn't work, you didn't eat. We all worked. I had an uncle, Richard Thomas, my mother's half brother, I loved him. There were few families that didn't have half brothers and sisters or step brothers and sisters but we never differentiated between us. We were all family. Uncle Richard would ask us what part of the chicken we wanted and he would not eat that piece. He would leave it on the platter for us.

He always ate before us. The working adults always ate first. He would always ask if I had helped Gram'ma 'Liza, and she would say how I dusted or helped her with the 'white folk's laundry.' I remember his smile. We always had enough meat and vegetables piled high on the table.

Uncle Richard worked for the railroad. At noon it was my job to take him his lunch. Gram'ma Liza would fix chicken and vegetables or beans and always in a mason jar, she poured lemonade with ice. Sweet lemonade. He would let me have a sip sometimes.

Oh I had a great life in New Bern. I loved it. I had responsibility but I felt loved, wanted, needed, and cared about. Sometimes I would cry when I had to go back to Boston. I remember once I tried to hide so that I wouldn't have to go back. Finally, Gram'ma 'Liza talked me into going back to 'help my mother.' My Gram'ma was named Eliza Jane. We always tried to style her hair in European-American styles, curls and such. The last time I saw her she had two plaits (braids), one on each side of her head, Native American style.

I loved my Gram'ma "Liza. Every summer, my brothers and six other grandchildren and I landed on her door step. Next door and so close by was Gram'ma Rose. She was not related to me but was the maternal mother of my cousins' mother and a Lumpi Native American. She was short and also wore her hair in plaits.

I remember leaving the house and having the screen door slam. "'Who slammed the door?"

"'I did Gram'ma'," I replied.

"'Do you live in a barn up North honey?'"

"'No ma'am."

"'Do you have doors?'"

"'Yes ma'am."

"'Well, honey, down here we close doors, we don't let them slam. Now you go back and open and close that door.'"

"'Yes, ma'am.' I learned from this beautiful woman who never went past the third grade about caring and giving love, manners and morals, correct speech and stamina.

She never raised her voice in all the time I remembered her. I never heard her holler at any of us. She only spoke once to tell you to do something. You moved or her slipper would come across the room to catch your attention. She believed if you spared the rod, you spoiled the child. Only her rod were the switches she made us pull off of the vines and trees, if we needed to be reminded whose house this was and who was the final authority. There were no spoiled children around her.

I remember my younger cousin coming in the house and asking me, "Anyone in the bath room?" In my Northern,

Boston accent, I replied, "No one is in the b<u>aa</u>th room." When she finished using the facility, she slowly descended the stairs with her hand on the railing, saying, "No one's in the baaaaath room." She repeated it several times. Lesson heard and lesson learned. I never wanted to be viewed separate from my Southern training. I spent many years as a public speaker and lecturer. I have made it a point not to sound like a Northerner with a Bostonian accent. In fact many people are surprised when I say that I am from Boston. They often reply, "'you don't sound like a Bostonian."

The Sitting Lesson

I remember Gram'ma 'Liza had told all of us girls how to sit when we wore skirts. We were to sit with legs crossed at the ankle, knees always together. My cousin Edna had a habit of sitting with her skirt up on her knees, leaning over with her elbows so you could see up her dress. Her excuse was that it was too hot to keep her legs closed. One day we were sitting on the back steps, and Gram'ma 'Liza was coming up the walk to the back door. We all greeted her and she smiled. She greeted us and never said a word to Edna. She went into the house, took out a tray of ice cubes, put them in the pitcher, added water, and came back outside. Without any word or warning, she threw the ice water up Edna's dress. Needless to say Gram'ma 'Liza never again saw Edna sitting in a skirt with her legs wide open, no matter how hot it got.

She told me she was born on a reservation. I used to ask her about her life on the reservation. Her only response was, "'Chile, I don't like to talk about it. There was so much killing and murdering and war. I don't like to talk about it." And she never did to me. I wish she could have told me more.

One God

I remember when I joined the Nation of Islam. I went down South to tell my Gram'ma to stop eating pork, how to feed, kill and clean chickens, and how to eat to live. I was the anointed one, come to save my loving Gram'ma 'Liza. After all my rambling about Jesus, God, and Allah, she looked at me lovingly and said, "'Do you believe in One God?"

"'Yes ma'am."

"Then that religion is all right."

That was it. She said nothing else. Then I remembered how when I was younger, she would pray over chickens before they were killed; or how she would keep them off the ground days before she killed them; or how people would ask her to pray with them or call her when someone died. My uncle said she was a Native American holy woman. I know everyone respected her and I never heard a harsh or evil word spoken to her or about her. She was a woman of few words.

Sam McCotter

I learned she had been married several times. Her surnames were Jones, Thomas, and McCotter, misspelled McCarter by the town clerk. Her last husband, Samuel McCotter, was an ex-slave from Pamilico County, North Carolina. He got some acreage and she married a man of substance. They used to call him Crazy Sam.

As the story goes, at night white people would come and move the markers on his land, and he would shoot at them. Needless to say, they thought him crazy and left him alone. When I did research on him, I found that he and some others had thought that they had purchased a parcel of land to build a school. After much hard work, they built the school only to have it suspiciously burned to the ground. When they started to rebuild the school, they found that legally they had only bought the right to build one school and had never purchased the land. They trusted the people to deal in good faith. They could not build the school, and so they lost all that time and money. In that day, for slaves or ex-slaves, that was a travesty.

Concerning their marriage, the story goes, that one day Sam McCotter raised his hand to hit my Gram'ma 'Liza and she turned on her heels and walked out the door, leaving him with thirteen children. No man was ever going to beat her. The next day while he was in the fields, she returned, took her children out the window and never went back to Pamlico County. She went to New Bern, North Carolina, just up the road. She never got a divorce and he married and had several other children.

Dear Holy Spirit, I thank you for giving me Eliza Jane as my grandmother, my guide, mentor and my example. When all around is 'sinking sand', she showed me how to be as the Rock of Ages. I

*would have faired better had I followed her true example, but I am
so grateful for having her in my life.*

My Mothers' Birth

What I learned of my mother is that she was born pre-
maturely. In 1917 there were no hospitals for Coloreds' in the
South, and as such none in New Bern. My grandmother put my
mother in a shoe box and kept her near the stove. She survived
and was the last child to die when she passed away in 1996.

My mother was a believer in justice and thus was a fighter.
People tell the story that a white insurance man came to the
house once a month to collect a dollar for my Gram'ma's insurance policy. One time he came by and had words with my
Gram'ma. Whatever the words were, my mother didn't like
his attitude, and she spoke up. He snatched the money and
said something that made my mother pick up the brick that
was lying by the door, used to hold the screen door open, and
hit him upside the head. He survived, but that night they say
my mother was on the Cadillac junket heading north to New
York. I understand a group of white men came by looking for
her but they never touched Gram'ma 'Liza because everyone
knew her and respected her. If they had touched her, I am
sure all hell would have broken out in that community. That
is how my mother came to New York and finally to Boston.

I was probably a prime target for the Nation of Islam. I
had experienced the white man's justice and hate. A childhood friend of mine, William (Fred) Shepard, was shot in
New Bern because he would not get off the sidewalk when

a white girl walked by. I remember him to this day, with his lazy eye. When it happened the black community shut down. The women were told to stay in the house, and the men did something retaliatory that forced us to stay off the streets and not go in town for a few days.

In the South every boy received the gift of a BB rifle his ninth or tenth year, and by thirteen or fourteen they carried a gun with shoulder holster. That was normal.

Mothers' Pain and My Gift of Song

My mother was not affectionate to me. The family gatherings were always held in my absence. When I lived in Maryland, she would call me the day before the affair, even though she would have let my brothers know weeks in advance. But when a crisis came, she would tell everyone to call Thelma, because she can straighten it out. I loved my mother, but I learned early that you could not dictate how a person will love you. I believe she loved me, but she had her own crosses to bear. The day she died, she told me she never wanted me, but God had let me live to do something great and please take care of my brothers.

That's the story of my life, being responsible for others. My brothers should have been looking out for me, taking care of me. Is there something wrong with this picture? Well Ma, we'll see what Divine Spirit will allow me to do, and I persist in helping others.

So after leaving the building, of the Temple, not my faith in the Creator, I began to pursue careers in both education and social service. Because of my experience as an educator, activist and business owner, I was called on many times to lecture. I was the head speaker for an ITT graduation. At the end of the presentation I sang, *Don't Liberate Me and Hate Me.* An original song of mine. I was called on many times to lecture because of my so-called 'standing ' in the community. I started singing at the end of my speeches and orations, even at my graduation from Antioch, which later became Cambridge College. I believe you never throw away a gift from God. Some day I will do a total music performance and maybe even with the Boston Symphony Orchestra. You're never too old to dream

Chapter V – The Marriage

Life with my Husband

In January 1962 I married a Muslim man, or so I thought. He had been married before to a woman of the same name, Thelma. She died of leukemia. I had been told by the Honorable Elijah Muhammad, himself, to marry my equal or better. So when I considered marriage, I had a house, he had a house; I had a car, he had a car, I was a Muslim, he was a Muslim. Enough said, I would grow to love him! How naive I was. I had never been out in the world and in my daughter's words, "'You didn't know N*****s, of all colors." You never give wisdom to a child, a baby or a fool without continuous ongoing guidance. I was at least one of those.

Brother Ralph recommended my former husband as a good brother. Ralph was a good brother and I trusted his judgment. My former husband was quiet and always smiling, such a lovely smile. He was quiet around me, so I thought, he seemed nice. Everyone encouraged me to meet him, and so I did, and then I married him. "You'll grow to love him'" that was the word handed down. In Islam, you must understand that our dating was chaperoned. We were never alone until we married. I never kissed him until after we were married. No one told me that he had beaten his first wife or that he had been given time out of the Temple for smoking. It was the culture in our training that you could not drink, smoke, fornicate or commit adultery. If you did you were honor bound to inform the community and you were removed until you could return among those who were striving to live within the discipline. *Time out* of 30, 60, 90 or more days was given for not conforming. I married what I thought I saw: a humble, righteous, hard working, and God fearing man. I was inexperienced, looking for others to guide me. I was neither typical of an American female nor African American woman of the 60's.

We got married by the justice of the peace, not because I didn't want a wedding but because the marriage my mother had planned I could not afford. We discussed back and forth about who to invite and, who was going to pay for the wedding. She had never had a wedding, and I had to have one just to let people know that I was a virgin. I was tired of the ongoing hassle. The day I left my mother to go to my new husband's house, my mother looked down the steps and said, "Now don't you beat her.'" He turned and said "What kind of brother do you think I am? I would never do that.'" I was off to a wonderful marriage, I thought. I waited for this first night of conjugal bliss. I just knew I was in the "happily ever after" zone.

We arrived at his home and I turned to him with open arms and said, "I love you." He said, "Yeah", but didn't touch me and then said, "Go take your clothes off and get in the bed, I'll be right back.'" I was shocked and bewildered. I just stood there wondering what had happened to this smiling, attentive, and loving man I thought I had just married. He went downstairs to the basement, and when he returned he smelled different. By then I was emotionally comatose. I kept trying to understand what had I gotten myself into. The marriage was consummated. I felt like I was a thing. There was no happily ever after.

The next day he brought me flowers. I thought then that I must have over-reacted. Things were going to get better. Over the next several months I got to know the man I married. Unfortunately I quickly learned that the beautiful smile and the constant brushing of his teeth was to take the smoke and marijuana smell from his lips. How could I have known? He had wanted children because his first wife couldn't have them, so I planned to marry at a time I knew I was fertile and offer to my husband my love and ability to birth. Isn't that what I was born for? Well yes and no. I kept asking myself that question. Wasn't I born and trained to serve my husband? Wasn't this the marriage that I had prayed for? Nothing could be as bad as I thought it was. I must have been over reacting.

Pride made me stay. I had no one to turn to. Gram'ma "Liza had passed. I tried to talk to my mother, but in her eyes he was a man who worked and had to be good. I had no confidants but Malcolm, and I was ashamed that I hadn't been wise or experienced enough to see through this façade. No person should marry on the basis of a smile, a recommendation. I didn't do my research. There was no marriage counseling because we were all walking the Islamic path, or so I thought. The information was there but I listened and trusted others. I was naïve. I was devastated.

Then I speculated, maybe this was what God wanted for me. This was the real trial in my life to see if I could be a good mother and wife to a black man. After all, hadn't I learned of all the trials of the black man, how he had been kept down and destroyed by the white man? It was up to us black women to restore their confidence, give them back their rightful place in the world. It wasn't difficult to convince myself that I had a role to play and a job to do, to assist my husband to find his place in the world.

Hadn't I gone to college? Didn't I have all the advantages? Wasn't this my calling? I convinced myself that my marriage was my final test of womanhood. One can formulate pseudo-happiness; I didn't remain with my husband because I loved the situation. I had three children; I never wanted them to come from a divorced family. I did it because I understood duty and responsibility and I had convinced myself this was the real plan for my life.

In 1969 we started a family business of installing glass in windows. The company grew from our efforts until we could hire three men to assist him on the truck. It was called AA Glassmobile, Inc. For awhile, it was the main source of our income. This was to become a success, and, ultimately the cause of the destruction of the marriage. I'll talk more about this later.

As I look back, I wonder how I ever survived. I honestly didn't know how marriage would be or should be. I fantasized, like most young girls about the joy of marriage, but my life was duty. I accepted it and having never received expressions of love in my life, I didn't expect more. Except for three lovely children, I consider my marriage a learning lesson in what not to do. I lost babies because my husband believed that "if you beat them in the stomach, it doesn't leave any marks."

In the sixteen years of marriage, I lost one baby at five months between my sons. The doctors said she would have been a vegetable. I would have lost my second son but I had my womb tied until his birth. I lost four or five more early in the pregnancy. I made the decision to use contraception on my own. I was told Muslims didn't use contraception. I did. Ten years after my second son, I thought I could live with the life I had made and I had a daughter.

I left several times, only to return because of the children. I wanted them to have a father in the home. One time when I left, I started to get in the Cadillac he had bought for me. My husband told me, I was not taking anything out of his house. I walked to the corner and hailed a cab. I left the house, the business, the children, everything. He wanted it all, it was his. I could take no more of this marriage. I wanted out. I caught a cab and went to a hotel. He said he would never come and get me. Well, he followed the cab until he found where I had settled. He had everything he wanted, and I was afraid, tired and desolate. Within twenty-four hours he was calling and asking me to come back. We were going to work it out.

I wanted to save my marriage, and he agreed to go to counseling, but the counselor had to be a black man. We found a black man who was blind. My husband was ecstatic. He might have been blind but he was not stupid, and he had fantastic insight. As the drama played out, the counselor would say, "'Do you understand what he is saying Mrs. Moss?' Do you hear him?" It took awhile, but I finally realized that there would be 'no happily ever after, not even close.'

My father-in-law came from West Virginia. He was a deacon in the church and clearly believed that our union could be saved. He asked me to go to a church, any church to save my marriage. I agreed. When my husband returned from dropping him off at the airport, he informed me that no one was going to tell him how to live his life. We never went to a church.

No matter how much I encouraged him he wouldn't learn the administration of the business, nor go to meetings of the Contractors Association of Boston and Black Presidents of New England. He would leave everything for me to do and, dutifully, I did it. My life, if it was bad after that, became worse. By the time this happened I had three children.

I tried to talk to him about wanting space/timeout, but he viewed that as wanting to be liberated. He suggested I put all the bills in my name. I thought that this was his way of trusting me. I wrote a song called, 'Don't Liberate Me and Hate Me'. Just before we divorced, I was to later find out that with all bills changed into my name, he walked away free, with $25,000 dollars from a government loan, for a contracting job.

What made me finally decide to leave was when he knocked me down in front of my daughter. All the other times he had beaten me in private or at least after the children were asleep or out of sight. For whatever reason, I blanked out the beatings and the abuse as long as the children didn't see them. As a child, I had seen the abuse between my mother and father. I believed that if the children didn't see it, it didn't happen. I saw the look on my daughters' face, and just then I had a flash back of my mother and father fighting. So

I decided then and there I would leave. I had been wrong to stay so long. It had hurt the children and me, both physically and mentally. Hindsight is 20/20

After the counseling sessions and being beat in front of my daughter, less than 6 months later, he pulled a gun on me and told me I wasn't leaving. I called 911. I can still remember that night. He threw the gun away, out in the yard. The policeman looked at me crying and scared to death. He put me out of the room and talked to my husband. Then he sent him outside and called me into the room. His first words were, "'Lady that man is crazy. How long have you been married?" I told him. "I'm going to lock him up for the night. You go and get a restraining order in the morning. But if you ever let him in this house or go back to him, don't call me." Through teary eyes, I promised him and God that if I could get him out of the house and my life, I would never let him in again. I didn't.

God was still looking out for fools and babies, and He wasn't through with me yet. Thank you Divine Spirit for your guidance and protection.

Lillian the Third Wife

He left town and went to live in Ohio, remarried and started a new life. I encouraged my children to see him and his new wife. She was a beautiful woman, her name was Lillian. She called me once to ask about the behavior he was showing. She said to me that "you can show him, in black and white, the truth, and he would be adamant that what he thought or believed was the truth, and he would not deter from it." "'I know," I replied.

He hadn't changed. He had called me an unfit mother and made her believe that she could take of my children. By the time she realized that he had been lying, and was manipulative, they were married. They lived together for 16 years until she died. We interacted on many of my daughters' events, such as graduation, senior prom and other college situations.

We talked; I knew her pain and she maintained her marriage because of the children. She loved them. She was Seventh Day Adventist and passed while teaching Sunday School; such a lovely human being. To my knowledge, he never attended church, except for Lillian's funeral. So, for thirty-four years he had little or no interaction with his children. She was the mainstay in the connection to the children. I am sure her death was a tragic moment for all of them. With her loss, he lost the connection to his children, again. Lillian was the maintainer of birthday cards and telephone calls. He never knew their birthdays nor sent a card of acknowledgement, but he always knew their telephone numbers if he wanted or needed money. It was always about him, his view, and his needs. Lillian had prudently provided for him. The house would be paid off on her death and he was left with little or no bills to pay. He wanted to have money, however, so under the influence of family members, he remortgaged the house, and created a debt that, without a job, he would be responsible for.

I don't believe I have ever received any caring or love in my life. I received duty and responsibility from my mother and nothing from my father. When I married I expected to hear words like, "darling,'" or "I love you'" or see "a knowing smile', you know, all the things that little girls dream will happen with happily ever after." It never happened. No. That's not true.

On the day of divorce, my husband told the judge, "Your honor, I love my wife." After years of violence, physical and mental abuse, that statement didn't ring true and came too late.

Later in life I met, again with Brother Ralph, the brother who advised me to marry Willie, and to grow to love him. Brother Ralph apologized to me. He told me that he felt I would have had a positive influence on my husband.

Again, I thank the Creator God for guidance and protection, I lived through it and brought three beautiful children into the world, and I'm still standing.

Other Memories During the Marriage

In 1963, two mysterious men came to the house selling material, and had asked me what I was going to name my son, they offered three Muslim names. At that time I had a Muslim name all picked out, *Wahid Jamil*, meaning (unique, matchless; handsome and impressive) but his father won out giving him his name, Willie. In March 1965, my second son was born. Once again, two different men came by the house selling material and they gave me a choice of three Muslim names for my son. I wanted to name him Malcolm but didn't. My husband felt the retribution that might be heaped on him could be catastrophic. I choose Marwan, meaning (solid as a rock) after an Arabic general. After choosing the name I never saw them again. I wanted to name my daughter something special. I looked in books, Christian and Muslim, for a name befitting my only girl. I prayed and finally I saw the name, Nam'ala. The meaning was, 'wise, clever, intelligent, witty woman,' Namala, that was the name! To this day, I cannot find the specific book that gave me the name or its' meaning.

In February 1965, Malcolm X died, but like a sweet memory, no one can take away my brother, my confidant, or my friend. He has a special place in my life and memories. Malcolm X was a role model to me. He overcame the pain, hate and suffering of his youth and forged a life built on the intellectual use and understanding of words. This led him to exam himself and open up to a world of global possibilities. He is sorely missed.

I get upset when I hear children of any color or persuasions speak about what a great man he was and abuse his character and morals, by not following his example. It does not matter where you've been or where you are at the time, grasp education wherever you may find it to further yourself. If you can't read, learn, don't be embarrassed. He studied, even in prison. He searched for the truth, regardless of the influence of whom or what. Rest assured, if you truly seek, you will find. No excuses of birth, racism, or poverty will be accepted. We have preceded you, and you can make a difference in your own life and in others.

I went back to school at sixty-nine years of age. I studied and received an Associate in Biotechnology. Did the other students give me a raised eyebrow? Some did, but so what! Was it difficult and hard? No, it was new. Of course, you cannot be expected to grasp something that is new, quickly; some do others don't. I am dyslexic so it is difficult for me to absorb things like other people. Be persistent; it takes constant rehearsal and memorization. Start with one class, maybe English. Go back, learn, require the teachers to help you understand the subject, most of them will be happy to have willing students.

Remember, Malcolm was a male role model. No male of African American descent should be spending his time wastefully or in criminal pursuits. You have things to do, you have books to read and you have to become part of civilized society. Move to your God Consciousness.

Years later, my son Marwan was watching channel 2, PBS, and *The life of Malcolm X* came on. He saw me in the video as a part of the drill team. We bought the video. It was strange how the Nation of Islam was creeping back into my life after so long.

Malcolm and I have the same birthday, May 19th. He would call every year up until his death mostly on our birthdays but always to check on me. "Hi sis, how are you doing? Happy birthday." I never told him how miserable I was, but he probably knew. I was ashamed. I was in an abusive relationship with a light skinned man. I had made my bed and I deserved to lie in it. **It was totally wrong thinking on my part.**

It took me sixteen years to figure out that when things are **bad get out of the bed and make it comfortable, by any means necessary.** My divorce became final in May of 1980. My Muslim, Christian tenets of no divorce had become life— long principles I tried to live by. Now I had to create new rules and guides to live by, without prejudice and racism, and going straight to God, with no intercessor. Much of what the

Honorable Elijah Muhammad had taught me I did not understand until I had more experience in life.

In Islam, in my youth, I was ignorant of most things. As I grew in understanding, I realized that we were all ignorant of many things. We misinterpreted and refined information to reflect our personal understanding. One thing you learn as an educator is that in order to educate and teach, you go to what the student knows or where the student is ignorant. You start where the learner's lack of information is, not where the teacher's knowledge begins or ends. Being under the direct tutelage of the Honorable Elijah Muhammad and his wife, Sister Clara Muhammad, I was protected from much misinformation.

Once I learned to independently think, discern, reason and expand the information so that I could understand, I was garbed in a Spirit of Divine Consciousness. Some considered this the first resurrection but I considered these the days of our ignorance. We were looking for guidance from the knowledgeable, the wise and the perfected ones, and there really were none. We were all learning. I believe the information the Honorable Elijah Muhammad gave me was specific guidance for me. It carried me through many challenges. Many things took me a long time to understand, and much of what I was taught is still unfolding.

My spiritual journey to the Creator God, Parent God and Allah, the Christ that All Knowing Power that is Omniscient, Omnipresent, and the Source of everything, never left me to fend for myself, and I never left Divine Spirit. We may have been ignorant and possibly resurrected but we were given a plan to live by that worked, works, and when understood benefits both body and mind.

Elijah Muhammad was an example of _what you could become, if you trusted in the Creator God; not a saint, but just a better human being in a civilized society._

Many will judge him by different standards, but few will dispute the positive impact he had on people (at that time), and "humans" like me. A simplistic explanation was given to me by an Algerian named Yusuf. He said, "there are good people and bad people." While this is not a final explanation, because we are hopefully moving toward our good selves and our Creator; I am thankful to the Creator God that all of these people were in my life and crossed my path during my journey. I'm no saint but I believe I am a better person for having known them all.

The Lost Members, Malcolm and the Nation of Islam

In approximately 2001 or 2002, I was a substitute teacher at Beaver Country Day School, a private school. The 12th grade students were discussing Malcolm and the Nation of Islam. They saw the followers as lost with no knowledge of what they were doing. I said nothing and did not interrupt. Suffice it to say, I hope that students when reading about that time in history will consider this analogy. A different soil for different plants.

The soil our ancestors were planted in and the soil that we inherited had to be changed. It produced anger; hatred of self and others, it was demoralizing, and not conducive to physical, mental or spiritual growth. All the eventual religious teachings created intercessors between us and God. It eliminated the Spiritual cord directly to the Creator God. The teaching of the Honorable Elijah Muhammad exposed our deficiencies, our anger and hate because we had a common experience of those behaviors. However, he also exposed our history and our need for God consciousness. He knew that 'two things cannot occupy the same place at one time.' We had to let go of the anger and hate so we could change, if we wanted to move toward our God Consciousness. Our family had to encompass the world, if we were to participate in a civilized society.

It is like being in a classroom and the teacher is trying to teach a subject, some get **all** of it, some get **some** of it, some get **none** of it and others **twist it** to be what they want it to be. The few who I knew got **all** of it, and had full knowledge of what they were doing, and were not lost. We, as a culture of believers, were not in the public eye, never publicized, but we were carefully 'cleaning' ourselves to become acceptable in a civilized society and to our Creator.

The multitude of crimes and things that have happened in the name of Islam and any religion, in my opinion are fostered by those who understood **some, none** or **twisted the teaching**. There are many unexposed former members who understood **all** and moved into the civilized society, living a quality, God Conscious life, and became constant learners for self and family. In my opinion that was the basic teaching of the Nation of Islam, and a part of my journey

Chapter VI – Other Changes

The start of redirection

Muslim women were not supposed to work, but nine months after my first son was born, my husband got triple vision and couldn't work. So I went to work. You never know the twists and turns that happen in life to benefit you. With a white glove he would rub the wood and if he found dust, I was not clean enough, not living up to MGT standards. The constant berating that I was not clean enough; smart enough and good enough had begun to impact my self esteem, again.

I took a night job at a bank and rushed home to nurse my son. There was appreciation at the job. Someone acknowledged me, valued me. As simple as it seems, that was probably the beginning in my mind's eye of seeing a door to freedom. I began to find ways to protect myself from mental injury. I had been shut down in every area of my life except mentally. He always began our sexual activity smoking, cigarettes, joints or drinking. He never seemed to be conscious, caring or romantic. I was never satisfied because it was always about him. It was in and out, and then he'd pass out.

During those sixteen years, I started a family business, started a YWCA, administered a school system, went back to school, got my bachelor's degree from Boston University; then my Master's degree in Education from Antioch (now Cambridge College), started my doctorate and started Suffolk Law school. He refused to be married to an attorney or a Ph D. The atmosphere at home was too virulent. I left school on both counts. He might control my life and body but he couldn't control my mind. I would remember my Gram'ma 'Liza's statement that, "'what you have in your mind and head, can't no one take away from you." Or I would remember Malcolm's admonition, "Sister, there are no dumb Muslims. Have we not been told to read and gain knowledge, wisdom and understanding?"

My life outside the house and at home was as different as day and night. I didn't make friends easily. None of my peers ever came to my house, only the friends of my husband came over. I was ashamed of how I lived and my home life. My husband made my home a place for his smoking and drinking buddies and I tried to be upstairs or out of the way with the children so that I wouldn't have to deal with them.

Milton Academy

I have lots of memories. I was finally making enough money to send my son to Milton Academy. I had hoped that I could offer my children the best educational experiences of the day. I didn't realize that my husband was against it. After my son was enrolled, he finally informed me that the public school education in West Virginia was good enough for him, and he wasn't going to pay for a private school. I paid for the schooling out of my check. As with any parent, I wanted to participate in the life of the school, get to know the teachers.

I was offered an opportunity to learn handball from one of the teachers. When I told my husband, he informed me that he would beat me if I did. I never learned to play handball.

My son was a good football player. One day his father came to the school drunk and confronted the sports director who was a former marine. He bellowed his prowess. The marine said, "Bring it on,'" and my husband left. Our lives now became a living hell. Anything said about Milton Academy was an anathema. One day there was a heavy snow storm, and my son had spent his money in school, had no money for the bus and walked home from school.

Of course he was late. I was worried and his father was drunk. When my son came home, my husband threw him through a wall for being late from school. When I finally asked him why he did this to our son, his response was, '"At least it wasn't a brick wall."

Our dogs

The children and I loved animals, and always had dogs coming into our yard and we would care for them. One day their father came home with another dog, a huge beautiful Saint Bernard. The dogs loved the children, and I could put the children in the yard with the animals and not worry about someone bothering them. My husband hit the boys for some reason, one day; the Saint Bernard turned on him, and the next thing I knew, that dog was gone. Over the life of the family we had Ralph, a puppy gift from my sister-in-law Bobbie; Sheba, half wolf and German shepherd, Bruno, half

Rottweiler and great Dane. He came to our garage, bruised and in pain. We nursed him back to health and fed him. He wouldn't leave. The last dog was Cato, full Rottweiler, a beautiful puppy. Marwan trained him.

One day I was in the backyard digging up the dirt in my garden to get ready for planting. It was a warm day and Cato was lying on the driveway in the sun. A neighbor who would always tease the dogs when he walked by came down the driveway. "I been hearing all this noise coming from the back. What you doing back there?", he said. I forgot the gate was open, but the signs were always posted, 'Beware of Dog." Cato jumped to his feet and headed up the driveway. All I could say was, "Run." Cato ripped off the pocket and attached material of his overalls to the skin. I grabbed Cato and closed the gate. I called the police, on the advice of my son. They came.

My neighbor talked about suing me. The policeman asked him if he could read the sign. He nodded his head, yes. They asked him if he had been invited on the property. He shook his head, no. The police man handed him his torn material and suggested he sew it back on his pants. I felt sorry for him and gave him ten dollars. My children disagreed. They felt that I should not have given him anything.

My signature is who I am

I remember the time that I started using my given name to sign my reports and letters. I was the executive director of the Experimental School System in Education of Massachusetts. I was responsible for writing reports about our work and its benefits to the other school systems of the state, as well as making reports to the Massachusetts Legislature. My boss, Dr. Anrig, who was the Commissioner of Education called me to his office one day and asked me why I never signed my letters or reports with my own name. I always signed things as Mrs. Willie J Moss. He asked me what my name was. I thought he was kidding me. "'It's Thelma of course." "'Why don't you sign the reports as Thelma Moss? Then underneath as Mrs. Willie J. Moss."

Honestly, I had never thought of that. My identity had been culled by my marriage and my religious training. Surely it was no problem to sign reports that way. Then, I thought, why shouldn't I give my father credit as well? So I started signing my name as Thelma Cromwell-Moss, and underneath in parenthesis, Mrs. Willie J. Moss. I was fine with that and Dr. Anrig was fine with that, but when my husband finally saw it, all hell broke loose. Who did I think I was changing my name? What gave me the right? I stood there traumatized. What had I done so bad?

The signature was really me together but separate. Then it finally dawned on me that he was living his life vicariously, through me. He boasted to others of what I was or what I had done, but was not holding up his half of the marriage by participating in the overall guidance and growth of the family.

Once, while I was head of the Experimental School System, I tried calling home to contact my husband. The janitor saw concern on my face and asked me what was wrong. I told him I was trying to contact my husband and I couldn't reach him. "Oh, I know where he is. He's around the corner at the bar.'" I walked around the corner only to find my husband in a shirt and jacket setting up drinks for everyone. He was doing this at a time when he was supposed to be working with the men on our business truck doing glass and glazing. He had said that he wasn't making any money on the truck. So I was forced to use my salary to pay bills, pay the men and keep the family together.

The Image

Everyone believed what I had portrayed, a lie, an ideal family and a loving husband. So it was difficult then to turn around and say that everything was not okay. Probably the worst part was having him tell all our friends and people that we knew that "you know how educated black women are. Their men don't have an education, and they beat up on them. These educated black women, man they are something else.'" The sad part is that family, friends, and everyone believed him. I had no one who would believe me. My mother saw a man that worked, "Thelma, he works, and you should keep him". I told her, "soon he'll be free, if you want him you can have him." In response to all of this, I became bitter and angry.

Like the Beth Israel experience, I had set the rules in play and the image was undeniable. I was the one who didn't understand the consequences of my actions. I was the liar and the villain. During the counseling I learned what I had been doing to myself and my children. I was an accomplice in this sham. I wanted out.

I remember we had just gotten a government loan of $50,000 to do a construction job. He walked into the bank, as treasurer and took half of it out. The president of the bank called me to ask what was going on. I had the account frozen. He went back the next day to clean it out, but he couldn't. However, with the remaining $25,000, the contract was successfully finished, unfortunately my family, the real workers, received no remuneration.

As long as he was in the house, each child went to his or her room and closed the door. When he left, the children opened their doors. I felt it was a sign. We could stop living in fear. I also thought that he would never see his children go hungry. Stupid me! I sat by the window waiting for him to drive up with food. I waited, until all the food was gone.

I remember going to the bathroom and looking in the mirror and asking God for help. I kept asking, "'Why? Why is this happening? Why would he do this?" The answer I received was "*it is*." Live in the present; see things as they are and not how you want them to be." Two simple words, '*it is*.' Whenever I feel that things are right or wrong, good or bad, I remember, '*it is*', and I can release the judgment analysis, and be accepting.. At that time something said to me, "'You have an education, your health, and strength, what more do you want?" Like dawn breaking over Marble head, I knew what I had to do, provide for my children. I humbled myself, dressed and went to the welfare office.

I explained the situation to the intake person and she immediately gave me food stamps. My sons were embarrassed to go to the store with food stamps. We finally agreed if I got the food, they would bring it into the house and put it away. For weeks we lived from hand to mouth, while I tried to figure out what I was going to do. Then, maybe ten weeks later, *a man* came to my door dressed in new clothes, sporting a suntan and wanting to see his children. He walked past me and went to the refrigerator, saw all the food there and declared, "I see you got food. I guess you got money.'" To this day I never told him that I was on welfare. He didn't care, and I cared less.

Saving My Home after the Final decree in May 1980

After the divorce, I met good men, and men I wanted to marry, but didn't. My children were scarred. I had sons who were ready to kill, because their anger was so great. I didn't have enough inside to offer. I had seen men try to chastise other men's children and the strain on the marriage that it brought. I was not up for that. One of my sons who had been thrown through a wall by his father, had bench pressed his way to a fifty-six inch chest, and bulging muscles. No one was ever going to hurt his mother again. The rage and pain in the children and in me were nothing a woman could put on a man she cared for or loved. I believed I had to do this alone. These were my children, and they were not the responsibility of another man. Though their father was ordered to pay child support, he never did. I figured if he could live with it, I could live without it. I would never put my children through what my mother put me through, just to receive child support. I worked and gave my mother my money just so I wouldn't have to hear her tell me about my father, and how she had to go to court to "get' money so we could survive. I refused to chase after a man who could have provided for his children, and wouldn't.

In the divorce, I refused alimony. I had an education, I could get a job. I expected the business would go to him, and I would keep the children. We had two houses. I expected each of us to receive one. The judge thought differently. He gave me the two houses, the business and children. He also wrote into the divorce decree that their father was not to see his children until he had cleaned himself of the drinking and drugs. I told the judge, '"You can't do that. These are his children." He said, "'Watch me." I thought that was harsh. These were his children and they should always know their father, no matter what he was. The judge did not agree.

I began to see the manipulative and devious side of my ex-husband. He had both houses, the one the children and I lived in, and the one we owned previously, designed to abort the court decree. He was successful in selling 37 Wolcott Street to a former brother-in-law. One day my son called to me about people standing in front of the house, as if reviewing it. I learned that the Federal Small Business Administration (SBA) was foreclosing for non payment; related to the money that he had taken before he left town. I called the SBA and they wanted payment or the house.

On the day of the auction, I explained to the auctioneer the situation I was in. The Saperstein Auctioneer refused to auction off the house and my younger son was able to assist in securing funds, and we negotiated a settlement with the SBA for 62 Richfield Street.

When I acknowledge a Divine Force guiding and assisting me through this time in my life, I know of the presence of Angels and a Divine Spirit. There was the auctioneer, and I was given children who stayed and helped me with very little grumbling because we were in this together, for survival. Thank you, dear Holy Spirit.

Chapter VII – Special People in My Life

Muhammad Asad

During 1983 and I am not sure how it started, I began to communicate with Muhammad Asad, an author of a Qur'an. He was a Polish Jew, (Leopold Weiss) who converted to Islam. He forwarded a copy of his interpretation of Qur'an. Instead of calling it a 'Holy Qur'an,' he called it, 'The Message of Qur'an.' The initial inscription reads, 'For people who think.' He autographed it in 1984, *'For my sister in Islam, Thelma Cromwell-Moss, with the hope that this Book will provide an abiding guidance for her. M. Asad 1/9/84.* This was my Islam. He gave me a Muslim name, Maimouna.

When I was working as a temp at the International Monetary Fund (IMF), I met Egyptian brothers. I asked the meaning of the name. They told me it meant trustworthy. Not just a person who was trustworthy but one whom even God trusts. Of course I was ecstatic. I mused, *'One who even God trusts!'* I vowed to make sure I never displeased the Creator, so that He would always trust me. However, later I learned that the name meant *'woman of destiny.'*

My mother had taken the surname Shakir, which means, servant of God. Her Muslim name became Amatullah Sabreen Shakir; My eldest brother became Abdul Kareem Shakir and my name was Maimouna Sabreen Shakir. They changed their names legally, I did not. If a name can identify you, then I want to have a name that considers my whole life. I would prefer a merging of histories that developed and fostered who I am and not eliminate my important past. I still have to deal with that dichotomy.

Maybe fuse together Maimouna-Thelma the first name and Grace-Sabreen, the middle. I wrestle with this but I know I will be guided when it is time. *I thank you Dear Holy Spirit for allowing Muhammad Asad to cross my path. You always send me reminders of your mercy and grace. You have supported and guided me irrespective of what name I use. I am so grateful for your Divine Guidance and protection.*

The Brahmans

Following the example of my grandmother, my mother and the MGT & GCC (Muslim Girls Training and General Civilization Class), I wanted to be a good mother. Before marriage, I had committed myself to being a good mother and never, under any circumstances would I divorce. Sometimes you speak errors into your future. You become committed to an idea that is destructive.

Belief in an idea at five years of age and that same belief at thirty years of age is not a rational process. Times change, situations change, and you change. Being stiff and straight, you are susceptible of becoming broken; being flexible and attentive to change, you can grow. I was close to being broken because I wanted my husband to be the man of my dreams, the man the Honorable Elijah Muhammad was molding and remaking. Finally, I had to accept the reality, he was not, and never would be the husband or father that I had expected from the men in Islam.

I studied Montessori Teacher Training to understand what I thought was the best training in education at the time. I became a teacher trainer. My children were playing instruments and learning Spanish and French by the time they were two. I lived in the ghetto, and I was concerned about who my children associated with, so I set about creating a band with children from the community.

The band consisted of six young men, my sons, Willie and Marwan, played bass guitar and synthesizer; my nephew, George was the lead singer; Wilson, a Hispanic, played drums; Tony, (nicknamed 'Poopie') a Portuguese, played guitar and Domingo, a Cape Verdean, played guitar. They practiced in my basement, garage or yard. They were excellent.

Whenever the neighbors heard them practicing they would stand at the fence and listen or if they practiced in the yard, the girls would be there. They played in schools, prisons, nightclubs, social centers and at community affairs. They opened for Patti LaBelle when she sang in Franklin Field, Dorchester. I helped them with home work and anything that I could to keep them from becoming another male urban statistic.

I came home one evening from a "'gig'" to find my two year old daughter reeling from drinking beer and her father and friends laughing and offering her more. I went insane, how could he, when I was working so hard to help our sons. Well, it was then I decided that maybe I shouldn't be out there managing the boys. Maybe that was a fathers' job, and I belonged at home. I turned the management of the group over to their father. After a while, things went sour, and the group disbanded. Later there were marriages and divorces. The only one I am aware of who has maintained his craft is my son Willie who has progressed on all string instruments and plays a "'mean'" seven and/or nine string bass guitar with excellence.

My Children

They are certainly a part of my journey. Were it not for my children who supported me, by Divine Permission, I could not have made it. They struggled with the loss of their father. They stepped in and became the guardians to their sister. They protected her. They helped me with the construction businesses, and tried to protect me, too. I guess you can say we were dysfunctional but we made it "through the rain" and I am happy to say they make me proud to be their mother. Maybe, someday they will write their stories, from their perspective. They have many tales to tell, I'm sure.

You were five, fourteen, and sixteen when I became a single parent and these were the most difficult years of my life. I had no road map, no blueprint, no family support and you were the 'wind beneath my wings', my reason for moving forward. As a single parent, I was focused, authoritative, scared, and full of love.

Willie, you took on the role of parent (father) and helped raise your brother and sister. You lost your youth, which can never be returned. You were outstanding. My prayer is that you are allowed to prosper in your music and have a life you deserve. Marwan, you were the person that saved our house on 62 Richfield St. Even though later I returned your money from an accident I had; it would never have happened without you. You will be blest for your efforts. Namala, you suffered a parent who was totally focused on your protection.

These are some of her stories. My daughter was attending Sister Clara Muhammad's School. I was concerned that she was not receiving a broad enough education so I entered her into Latin Academy. There were two incidents that I had to deal with. She came home one day to inform me that 'If you smoked Marlboro's you didn't become pregnant.' What?

One day Marwan answered the telephone and a young male student from Latin Academy was calling to talk to my daughter. He informed the caller that she did not receive male phone calls. She was twelve years old, which was my rule. The young man on the phone insisted and must have said something that infuriated my son. Who informed the caller that he would come through the phone and rip out his lungs, or better still he would meet him the next day at school. The boy never showed.

Then I was called to have a psychological evaluation meeting because, 'My daughter needed space.' The theory was that she needed to be more sociable. She was twelve years old; quiet, reserved and kept to herself. The teachers felt this was not healthy and unacceptable. While I might not disagree with them, I took into consideration where I lived, her choice of friends and the time to monitor this phase in her life. I asked the group of teachers and psychologists, 'What does she need space for?'

As I listened to their reasons for my daughter needing space, it became clear to me that they wanted to participate in the rearing of my daughter. So I asked, 'Which one of you wants her?' They were not sure what I was saying. Again I said, 'Which one of you wants her? Who will clothe her, feed her, and give her space until she is eighteen years old? And she better be a virgin and not pregnant when you finish. Who wants her?' I had no takers. Then as my mother before me, I informed the group that it was my house, my rules. I lived in the ghetto, no twelve year old daughter of mine was going to date, have male friends over my house and she was not going to theirs.' Right or wrong, clearly things were getting out of hand. As I was leaving, the psychologist pulled me aside and said, '"Ms Moss, you are absolutely right. I would have said and done the same thing in your situation. I was just doing my job." We shook hands and I left. I prayed for guidance.

Then my daughter asked to go to a private live-in school. My off-handed remark to her was, 'If you can find a school that is all girls and will give you a scholarship, you can go.' That Saturday we went to an educational fair where private schools were looking for students. By Divine Permission, she found a scholarship at McDuffy School for Girls in Massachusetts. I had given my word, so off she went to the private school. I visited often. One day while walking through the halls, I was asked if I taught there. "'I always see you here." "No," I replied, "my daughter goes here."

One day my daughter called me. She was upset because the counselor was meeting with all the other girls but not her. I made an appointment to meet with the counselor to find out what was the problem. I knew it could not have been race related because the racial diversity in the school was excellent. '"Ms Moss," she said, '"your daughter has a centered core. She can take care of herself. She only needs help with school work. She bathes, washes her clothes and irons. She is a role model for the other girls in that instance. I have nothing to counsel her for. You have done a great job as a parent. I will speak to her." '"No thank you, I will speak to her. Thank you." We shook hands

I left her office with such appreciation for all the difficulties I had gone through that now were starting to bear fruit. I talked to my daughter and explained the reason for her exclusion. She felt a lot better to the point that I later found out she had started her own little business charging to launder and iron clothes of the other girls. My daughter, the entrepreneur.

I knew this had to be the right decision at the time. I kept such a tight grip on her life and she needed to make friends and have space, but I needed to have some impact on where and when. McDuffy School was the ideal place.

Thank you, Dear Holy Savior. You gave my daughter breathing room and you removed a concern that I had. Again, Divine Spirit, you were helping me with decisions to aide my children. The twists and turns allowed her to become the good person she is today. I am so grateful.

For all my children, the concern was for your maturity, mental, physical and spiritual development. This was all done with love, maybe tough love but certainly love. You gave me the courage to press on with a smile, the balm that could sooth my soul and, with the Creator make another day. Through all of this you supported me in the construction company, at home, in school and in public. Our difficulty was a private matter. You may feel I caused you unwarranted pain. I can openly apologize.

I will never apologize for what all three of you have become because of and in spite of my actions. I am forever grateful for the prayers that preceded me and comforted me in this life. There must have been storages of love and prayers offered by my ancestors to carry me through this first phase of my life. Your Grandparents on both sides and my ancestors would be proud of where you are now.

Never forget the price paid by your ancestors. Never forget the Creator God in Spirit, by any name you choose; and never forget that this is your journey. Choose wisely, the consequences are yours. **No one is self made. We need each other; that is why we are here as a family, to make the journey bearable.**

When McDuffy school became coed, it was time to move on. Once again my daughter assured me she could find a school that would offer her a scholarship with education, room and board. She found one, Massanutten Military Academy in Massanutten, Virginia. A coed school. We went for an interview. Remember, I had no money, no reserve funds. I met the administrator of the school, Colonel Beck. He was kind and gracious, but you could tell he was a no nonsense military person. By then, I was hearing messages to 'let her go. She will be protected.' I looked at my daughter, '"This is not the place for you. Are you sure this is what you want?" Enthusiastically she said, '"Yes." I signed her up.

When it came time to go to the military school, I brought my mother with me so she could see where her grand daughter would be, at least, for the next year. We both agreed this was going to be more than my daughter had bargained for. If she thought we were controlling just wait until the Colonel explained his rules. Sure enough after one week at the Military School, I got the phone call. '"I want to come home." '"Sorry dear, you're there for at least one year, the length of the scholarship." She cried. I told her I loved her and hung up the phone. That was the hardest decision I had to make, but I knew for then, it was the right one.

I remember singing a song Gram'ma 'Liza loved. *"Precious Lord, take my hand. Lead me on, let me stand. I am tired, I am weak, I am worn. Through the storm, through the night, Lead me on to the Light, Take my hand Precious Lord, Lead me on. When the way grows drear, Precious Lord, linger near, when my life is almost gone, Hear my cry, hear my call, hold my hand lest I fall. Take my hand Precious Lord, lead me on:".* It reminded me that there was a Power that I could lean on.

She was fifteen. I had no regular full-time employment. I had left my sons in my Boston home expecting them to work in the non union house doing glazing, to continue their music, and maintain the home. When I returned, I closed the business. My eldest son, Willie, got employment at the Federal Reserve Bank, in security, while his brother tried to continue their music venture. They had built a professional recording studio in my basement and were writing and recording music. Young men need good, strong male role models. Unfortunately, there had never been any in their lives.

At this time they were twenty-four and twenty-two years old. I believed my sons were strong and mature enough to meet my expectations and handle the responsibility that I had left them. I was wrong. I expected them to maintain a house that needed constant maintenance, handle all the expenses for the studio and themselves, and work. I had been the hub, the center, directing every thing, now I was gone. I am sure they felt abandoned, first their father, and then me.

They survived my erroneous thinking and actions. They maintained themselves and as adult men have proven they can exert enough inner strength and stamina to meet the challenges of life. They have shown the capability to change, should they choose to, and if the situation requires it. My prayer is that they will choose wisely because there is still much to learn on their life's journey. Maybe they will learn by other peoples' mistakes. I hope so; it will save them much grief. Much of this they learned on their own. Like all of us, I hope they will observe that there is still much to learn on their journeys.

Were it not for prayer, the power and protection of the Creator God, I could have lost my sons. Thank you, dear Holy Spirit.

I moved to Maryland to live with my niece by marriage that had just lost her job in the airline industry. I thought I could help her as a change agent. Her story is found later. I believed I could still be close to my daughter, a two hour drive, if she needed me. I lived in Maryland for eleven years driving once or twice a month to Boston to check on my sons and mother.

My daughter flourished in this military setting. She rose up the ranks quickly. Colonel Beck gave me constant reports to allay my concerns. He was wonderful. Once again, people were put in my path to assist me, angels in human form. I tease my daughter, sometimes, that she shut down the Academy. It seems she had a boyfriend who was very protective of her. They were standing talking but I guess another young man was staring at her and she commented about it to her boyfriend. He wanted to know why the other boy was looking at her. The boy gave a remark that made her boyfriend punch him and the melee was on. It became a free for all.

I did not receive the first call from my daughter. She couldn't reach me; I was in a meeting, so she called my mother. My mother called me and I called Colonel Beck. I talked to my daughter; she was crying, upset and wanted to come home. I spoke with the Colonel, asking him if I should come down, as if I could do anything. He assured me that he could handle it. The school went on lock down; students were given the required military punishment and everything returned to normal. I eventually met her young man. I was sure he would protect her, but who would protect her from him, I thought. Once again, Dear Holy Spirit you had a plan that I did not know. He was her date at the military ball.

Starting her second year on scholarship, her grades and decorum were such that the Colonel was suggesting she graduate and go to a regular military academy. She was that good. But that was not to happen. The school was sold and new administrators came on. I had given my resume to Colonel Beck and explained my financial situation when I came to the school. These new administrators viewed my background in the North as elitist and demanded I pay full tuition. I had no money. In the meeting with the new group, they made snide remarks about Northerners, the Kennedys and it was clear to me, I had to move on. Their positions were pay or withdraw. So in the first quarter of her junior year, I withdrew her. I later understood Colonel Beck also left. Once again, the guidance and necessary changes were moving me down a path that I had not planned. We lived in Suitland, Maryland. I registered her in Potomac High School.

Because of the training at the Military Academy, she was advanced in most of the classes. By now my daughter knew me well enough to know that schools were a place for education and advancement not a place to wile away her time. She complained about two teachers. I removed her from a class where they watched movies all during class. I removed her from a class where the teacher literally read the book to 11th grade students. After talking with her, I knew she was racist. As in many school systems, you can't fire or replace teachers who have seniority and whose behavior is questionable. The administrators were wonderful. They understood my requests and supported my efforts.

This school was a predominately black student population and black administered. Namala thrived in this black community atmosphere. Like me, she had a foot in both camps; the South and the North and she survived and understood the nuances. She graduated and in her late twenties joined the Air Force with a waiver. When the officers commented how easily she accepted the military life regulations, she told them there was no democracy in her home when she was growing up. It was like the Mafia. Sometimes it hurts to hear that but that is her opinion.

During all this, I prayed and God never left my side.

I did not want my daughter to go into the service. She was grown and I could not stop her. The recruiting officer and I had words when he questioned her, was she going to listen to him or her mother. I not so politely informed him that I had known her for over twenty-five years. I got her to delay her decision. He called every day, sometimes twice a day at her job. Finally she came to me and told me she was going to sign up. I went with her as they laid out the 'opportunities' she would receive. I did not want her to go. She became a weatherman. I got no spiritual guidance on this; maybe I was too involved and wouldn't listen. She went; she deployed and was released with an honorable disabled discharge.

My prayers were with her all the time. Many times I cried and prayed for her guidance and protection. My prayers were heard.

Dear Holy Spirit, I am so grateful for returning my daughter; allow her to have the life she wants and deserves.

In the meantime, one son became a Boston policeman and the other remained at the Federal Reserve Bank. I write very little about them because I am still trying to rebuild a relationship that is haunted by my action or non-action in their lives.

Dear Holy Spirit, as they go through the challenge of seeing their father in ICU, allow them to let go of their pain and build their lives on the understanding that I did all I knew to do under the circumstances. Allow all three to become closer in your realm of forgiveness. Allow them to forgive themselves, me, and each other; allow them to build lives that make a tighter knit family based on love, joy, and happiness.

Chapter VIII – Being Me

The Roxbury YWCA - ASWALOS House

In the winter of 1967 I joined a mother's program at the Boston YWCA. It was a swimming class that allowed me to swim with other mother's, and arrange swimming lessons for me, with my sons. In 1968 the shot heard round the world was the death of Dr. Martin Luther King, Jr. I was with the mother's in a meeting when we heard the news. There was a solemnity of connected pain that we shared as everyone looked around the room at me, the only black member of the group. There were tears and a hollow empty pain in the pit of my stomach. I did know and cared about Martin. The women whispered and then someone suggested that the group do something to show the black community how they felt.

The suggestions ranged from having a small gathering at the YWCA in Boston to hiring a bus and bringing woman from the ghetto to the center on Clarendon Street. There was a sincere and open concern about wanting to let the Roxbury community know that they loved and respected Dr. King, as well as the black community. I spoke up and suggested that they put a YWCA in the area. Why should they have to come here to appreciate and participate in the programs? They agreed it was certainly a great suggestion. They suggested that Ms. Eleanor Strapp, the executive director come in and hear the suggestion.

We made the request and Ms. Strapp seemed to think that it was a nice idea. She thanked us for meeting with her and sharing our concern. Two weeks later, we met again and I asked the group what had happened about our suggestion. No one knew, so I met with Ms. Strapp to find out what was happening about putting a program in the Roxbury community. She informed me that she had no power to make that kind of decision; it had to be a decision made by the board. Someone in the group would have to go before the board of the YWCA and present the suggestion. I was that person. At the next board meeting, I was on the agenda. I met with a board of all white women. The one black member, Ms. Glendora Putnam, was an attorney. The most vocal person on the board was Virginia Ehrlich. She explained how her family had been a strong supporter of the YWCA and she believed that putting a program in the Roxbury community would setup a segregated program. "This will never happen in this YWCA. I have spent my life working for equality and desegregation. We will never support a segregated YWCA."

This was the sixties, and the thought of blacks meeting without whites participating was an anathema, segregation again. It was not conceivable that maybe blacks needed the experience to create, grow and develop organizations with the experience of the broader community, so they could have equal partnership and parity. I was surprised but undaunted; I continued to pursue the YWCA in Roxbury.

This was my first time coming before a group or a board that seemed to hold fiercely to a history and a belief that their way was the only way, and that people and life had not changed outside of the Boston YWCA's hallowed walls. This group had many God-centered, sincere women working within their experience. I dug my heels in and so did Virginia. We exchanged heated words at several meetings and finally one day she invited me to her home for lunch. She got to know me. We became friends. I then felt that the board would move forward to put this program in the community, and so my job was finished.

I met with Ms. Strapp and her assistant Evelyn. I told them that I was a Muslim. I explained that while I appreciated the trust they were beginning to give me, I felt that since it was a Christian organization and I was not a Christian, they could now find any good person to carry out this idea or plan. I will never forget her looking at me and saying that "we are a Christian organization, but we are open to women of every religious group and every ethnic background.'" I was shocked, but it was because of her statement. After all that I had been through to get the idea to the board, added to the national distrust and hate of "(Black) Muslims" at the time, how could they trust and support what was '"my dream," a YWCA in the minority community open to all women of the area?

I was given a challenge, Well, what to do? I contacted my neighbors, and they started supporting me. Then I met Mrs. Jimmie Bleckley. God bless her. She was older than I was and a strong, persistent, Christian. We went to the leaders of the community. She knew them all. They all refused to help. Their view of the Boston YWCA was an "elite" group of rich white women who hadn't the slightest idea of what was going on in the world, let alone the minority community. But Ms Bleckley and I persisted. Ms. Eleanor Strapp said, "If you can find 20 children in the community who want a program, we will consider it. However, we will not pay you for your efforts.'" "Fine with me," I said.

We finally got the Boston YWCA to set a date. They would give us $1,000 to do a summer program. We had the support of Ms. Helen Davis, the funeral director, who got us space in her church, the Eliot Street Church, Roxbury.

We had an older friend of Ms. Bleckley, Ms. Jackson who would look after the babies while the program was there for the young girls. The elderly women of the community rallied around me and we blanketed the churches and shops with our flyers. They offered to teach sewing, arts and crafts, cooking and any skill that they knew. On a Saturday, at Eliot St. Church over 150 girls signed up to participate in the YWCA programs. We could not serve them all at that time; we took names and turned many away. It blew the roof off the Boston YWCA mentality. There was a need, and we had proven it.

I felt such a relief, now I could go back to my family. This volunteering took much of my time. The Boston YWCA, would move ahead in finishing my dream which was now our dream. Virginia Ehrlich, who had vowed that no segregated YWCA program would ever exist now supported me, and became my best friend and strongest supporter and ally. I thought I was through. OH NO. They made me a member of the Boston Board. I was put on a Standing Committee.

I knew nothing of the workings of Boards or Committees. However, the Boston YWCA was the best learning experience and board process training one could ever have. Dorothy Height who was part of the National YWCA in New York came to Boston. She came to my house and shared a meal of meatloaf and vegetables. We talked about the YWCA and issues of the Black Community and her organization The National Council of Negro Women. I am sure that this was the first time Dorothy had eaten at a Muslim home, or talked with a so-called 'Black Muslim.' I loved her. She was the epitome of all the women of the South, the sustainers and maintainers of our community. She agreed to support me and my efforts. Well, all the dominoes were lined up. We had proven the need, and Virginia told me to go find a building. What did I know? I was passing a building on Seaver Street in Roxbury and saw a for sale sign in the window of a house on a corner. I told Virginia. The next thing I knew she had taken charge, gotten support for buying the house, "found" money to refurbish it, and championed my efforts, unbelievably. One thing I learned, is that, when women, black or white women, especially women with a cause, want to make something happen, watch out.

By then Ruth Batson was on the Boston YWCA board, and I was taken off the board and appointed the chair of the Roxbury governing committee of the YWCA responsible for drafting the by-laws and job descriptions.

What was driving me? Was I trying to set up another women's program, an MGT, No. I was going through my own personal hell, and I needed a YWCA. I believed that more than most women, we, minority women, needed breathing space. We weren't talking liberation from our men, as the women's movement was espousing; we were talking *'time out'*. We were taking *'time out'* from the chores, the babies, and even the husbands. We were finding some breathing room. Many of us worked every day and came home to keep house, and take care of our children and husbands. We were tired. We did not want liberation from our lives. We had sons. We did not want our sons to even consider that we hated men, or were trying to demoralize men. Our men were our leaders, partners, and heads of our homes. We viewed our liberation as a right to maintain and sustain our families and culture from an oppressive white male dominated power structure.

We weren't trying to change our culture, we were trying to expand our knowledge to include our culture, our husbands, and our children. We wanted to create our world, just as white women had created their world.

We needed time to think, expand our minds, even to dream of helping our husbands' and children without being constantly tired. Many of us lied. I lied. My Gram'ma 'Liza "hated a liar." I remember one time being intellectually and politically correct as I explained to her, "No, Gram'ma, you hate the lie not the person who lied". She looked at me as if confused. "A liar will tell a lie and another lie to cover the lie and more and more lies until he's caught and will still lie. If and when he stops lying then I'll watch him see if he changes his behavior and then decide to change how I feel about him." I had lied; I had lived a Dr. Jekyll and Mr. Hyde life. No one ever suspected I lived with an abusive husband for sixteen years. Shame stayed with me for a long time, but I digress.

Not all of us lived in abusive situations, but all of us always talked about how tired we were, getting up in the morning and at the end of the day. I believed if we had a place where 'so-called' upwardly mobile women could mentor their neighbors who were feeling distressed and depressed, we could begin to change the mother's minds. If we could change the mothers and how they viewed their lives, we could change our communities. Hadn't I learned that if we could put the family together, then the world would take care of itself! Hadn't I been able to fool everyone into believing I was happy by taking my 'time outs' at the Y? In a way, I was my own experiment, pouring my life into the community as an escape. Right or wrong, I was able to survive.

Well anyway I believed that, and that belief kept me going. I was always writing songs and poems. I wrote a song titled, 'Don't Liberate Me and Hate Me.' I sang it many times to groups, and at the end of many lectures. I still remember the positive responses to the song and lyrics. It hit a spiritual cord with other women. But let me stay on track.

I went from chair of the Roxbury governing board, to the chair of the Roxbury program planning, to the first executive director of the Roxbury Program of the Boston YWCA. My dream had taken shape and become a reality. I was a part of making it happen and watching it materialize. Sometimes I marveled at what had happened. Here I was a grand child of Native Americans and slaves and a child of divorce, having grown up with a single parent in the Mission Hill projects. I was a Christian, Catholic, Protestant, Pentecostal, Episcopal, (African Methodist Episcopal) AME Zionist. I was a "so-called' Black Muslim, who had put away race and hate, and was able to initiate something to serve the community. Certainly my ancestors and spiritual guides would be happy and satisfied with my efforts and I would go home. But then at the end of the day, I would go home to a life that was horrific, but it was mine, and the world would not have to know what I was going through. Not yet.

During my administration as executive director of ASWALOS House, a National YWCA convention was called in New York. Ruth Batson and I were sent to represent the ASWALOS House and the Boston YWCA. I listened to all the speeches about how we should come together as a national YWCA and eliminate sexism and racism and poverty and health disparities. I listened. Finally, I stood up and spoke. I remember ending with, "Since we know what we want to impact, why can't we agree to do it "By any means necessary." What a bomb shell! Fantastic. It was the mover of the convention. It was accepted. The rallying cry from then on and for two years was "by any means necessary."

The convention got turned around, and we women were free to think and create within our own capacity, "by any means necessary.'" When I finished my statement, I went upstairs and changed from my red suit to a different color. Everyone wanted to meet the girl in the red suit who had forged this unity among all the convention members. But in Islam, I had been taught that it was not acceptable to stand center stage to always be seen, it was not a woman's place. It was not the place to be. I wanted to make an impact to help people, to serve the community. I wanted to be remembered, allowed to make a difference and serve the broader community. That was a mental conflict, because sometimes the right message, from a change agent, at a point in time, puts one at center stage.

My life at home was very difficult so I poured myself into the program. The program and professional assistance from Ms. Strapp and her staff were unbelievable. She never left my side. She kept a polite distance but was always there to talk to, ask questions, and support me through the gaps in my knowledge. Ruth Batson was the community side, my board chair. Now we had to decide what to name this YWCA. Ruth Batson and I agreed to have a contest to name the center. The contest was open to school age children. We received a large number of suggestions, and we finally selected the winner. The winner was a little white girl who named the center ASWALOS HOUSE. While many might think it an African name, it was an acronym, All Sisters With A Lot Of Soul. This program, this house, this dream was truly becoming our home of impact, a community dream come true, or so I thought. Few people have an opportunity to see something in their mind flow to paper, and then become a reality. I am fortunate to have been one of those people.

I was young, innocent, and full of trust. The YWCA had protected me from the real world elements. The sixties was a time of minorities wanting to take control of their communities and destinies. Under the eyes of the YWCA board and a Roxbury YWCA governing board ASWALOS HOUSE became *self-governing* and *community controlled.* Given my history from the forties, the segregated south, and my background, as a so-called 'Black Muslim,' I felt honor bound to secure community control as part of the governing rules.

The black community must control its destiny; it was mature, and women were ready to work hand in hand with the Boston Board to serve our community, or so I thought. Naively, I pushed forward. I forgot the lessons of Beth Israel Hospital. I believed everyone who said that she had come to support ASWALOS House was on the same page as I was. Not so. The lesson was there, again. I felt like the bird that came down to visit the snake, and was bitten. Then a cow dropped dung on the bird so that its smell kept predators away and its warmth allowed it time to heal and survive the cold. I learned again that everyone that smiles at you is not your friend and everyone that drops dung on you isn't necessarily your enemy.

Our original committee members had changed. The initiators, the creators, the constructionists, and dreamers were mostly gone. A new breed of black women had arrived. They were well educated, politically astute, and the recognized leaders of the community. I am sorry to say, I never took the time to understand their vision of a Roxbury YWCA. Rightly or wrongly, I thought people were coming on board to help me expand my dream, our dream. But their dream was different. The statistics said we were a community of girls in trouble, welfare recipients, and single parents needing rescuing through government funding. That was not my belief. These new leaders did not see this House as their home but a place to put a government funded "program.'" Maybe they had the same interest but certainly they came at it with a different focus.

We had a board of black women governing ASWALOS House. Isn't that what I had pushed for? We were receiving funding from the Boston YWCA. The only thing I thought we had to do was serve the community. I thought I was a part of the community. I was informed that I was considered middle class. Clearly, I was politically naive.

In the South, we lived next door to one another and the elite were just as segregated as we were. The only requirement was that we be clean, go to church, be respectful, love and help others in the community. We didn't talk of classes within our community in the south because segregation made us equal. We all attended black churches, lived in black communities though culled in economic capability. We knew our neighbors and the network for assistance through the black community. There was a moral standard that superseded money, status, color and age. We knew the honest or honorable people and we knew the liars, "tramps," stealers, cheaters, and deceivers. We were a very close knit community. I was blind sided; I forgot this was Boston, a city that had yet to accept the word "black" in its' lexicon. Many blacks were still calling themselves "blue bloods."

I had come to build a community house but the word meant different things to different people. All black people or communities are not alike and do not think alike. I had not taken this into account. I did not consider the human element and politics. I soon realized that some people had come on the board not to serve the women of the community but for the prestige and power.

As executive director I had set up an agreement to receive $150,000 as seed money to be used to enlarge the building, have exercise rooms, sleeping quarters, and a place for unwed mothers. But the community board, these recognized women leaders of the black community, felt that my skills were not adequate to carry the "dream" forward, and I was relieved of my position. I guess the manner in which it was done was most disheartening.

One evening they invited me to the house of the wife of a minister who sat on the board. They told me that I would no longer be the executive director, and that was it. There was no reason given except that they felt I was not qualified to handle the seed money that was coming to the House. I was dumbfounded, but I guess I shouldn't have been. Hadn't I demanded that the black community control ASWALOS House? Hadn't I supported all the rules to make this House a service to the minority women of this community? I was shocked and devastated, but I had no recourse. I went on the radio and I tried every thing I could to tell my side of the story, but I had done my job too well.

Finally, I was brought into a meeting room, at the Boston YWCA, where they had a young black attorney, Wayne A. Budd. He informed me that the rules, as set down by the governing board had to stand. I had lost the right to finish my dream. Yes, I'll say my dream because these new persons had never put their personal blood, tears, or sweat equity into ASWALOS House. These women were in control, whether they represented the interests of the community, or not. They had status and connections and understood politics, and I didn't. In spite of my efforts to secure the seed money for the House, it never happened. They never got the seed money. Ruth Batson, a member of the governing committee at that time, tried to talk me through the process, and the politics. I just couldn't understand. She told me that I needed to understand politics. I thought that love of community and service to people was above politics, I was naïve, and probably still am. At the time of this writing, ASWALOS House is closed and the building sold. It grew, but it never grew to be the service that it could have been.

Ruth Batson called me to a meeting, several years later and asked me to once again champion the interests of the girls and women of the community. I met with a group of women and I was willing to work, once again to expand a center for women in the Roxbury Community. I put forth a possible course of action. I would use my contacts in the construction community to establish a committee of owners who might be willing to establish a women's' center. I would want to sell them on the idea of having pictures of their mothers' or grandmothers' encased in a circular hall called the "The Women Who Made Us." There would be plaques to identify the men whose females were responsible for their success and whom today were making Massachusetts a viable state.

After much discussion, a woman stood up and informed me that if Elma Lewis couldn't do things with her contacts, what made me think that I could do anything. I looked at Ruth, and she looked at me and sighed. These women wanted someone to show them how to make contacts in the government and in the wealthy community. I just wanted to empower women whether we had contacts or not. I was never involved in the YWCA again. I wanted to be involved, but what I had to offer was personal and involved sweat equity, not making programs that matched government funding. Money, government support, financial and growth opportunities would always come when you were trying to help yourself, I always believed that.

They tell me that the history of ASWALOS House has been written and put in the Schomburg Museum in New York. I hope they told the real story, how it really happened. How the women, uneducated, poor, with mother wit, love, and concern for their children, grandchildren, daughters and themselves forged a union with the Boston YWCA, in spite of their non-political prowess, and started a Roxbury YWCA, ASWALOS House. We were truly All Sisters With a Lot of Soul. They are the true heroines of ASWALOS House and the Boston YWCA. This is my story, and it never would have happened were it not for Virginia Ehrlich, Eleanor Strapp and staff, Helen Davis, Glendora Putnam, Dorothy Height, Ruth Batson, Mrs. Bleckley, Ms Cuthbert, Mrs. Jackson, Rubye Jackson, Gladys Diggs, myself and a host of neighborhood women in Roxbury and from the Boston YWCA, neighbors and friends. That was the history of ASWALOS House/Roxbury YWCA, as I lived it.

I saved minutes of meetings and wrote in my journals so that if ever I was confronted about this story, I could show what the minutes had to say. Malcolm X once told me, "If you don't write the history, others will make it up.'" I've met persons who tell a different story of their role in the founding of ASWALOS House/Roxbury YWCA. They have been awarded Paul Revere Silver Bowls for their involvement and accomplishments. I want the community and you children to know the truth. That was a poignant time in my life, a "time out,'" a Divine Spiritual experience and a time of change. I began to see my community in a broader sense, and understand how I had been groomed in Islam to think globally, not black and/or white, and these were diverging paths from what was now ASWALOS House. I just didn't belong to one side or the other, I had outgrown that thinking and had to move on.

Moving On

I learned also that nothing is forever. I was allowed to spearhead, initiate, and participate in the birth of a dream. Not many people get to do this. I was fortunate. They could take away control of what we women had built, but they couldn't take away our experience. We had built it; they were the newcomers who benefitted from our collective efforts. I had nothing to be ashamed of. Everything will and must change, I have learned as a natural law. I began learning how to let things go and not become attached to dreams or things. I learned to be like the bamboo that bends in the wind, and not be so "straight' and "strong' only to be broken by natural forces. I had people tell me that "I was a strong black woman.' I used to think that was a compliment. I grew to learn that it might have been a sign of my own unwillingness to bend. I detached myself from the YWCA dream and moved on to education and business.

Other challenges and opportunities:

➢ I served on Senator Ted Kennedy's Small Business Committee and with The Small Business Association of New England (SBANE). I helped to develop this group and participated as a representative in the First National Small Business Conference in Washington, DC;

➢ I started my doctorate at Antioch in Ohio, but was unable to finish;

➢ I attended Suffolk Law School and was unable to finish. I learned enough, with scientific help, to receive a patent for cleaning water. I did all the filings.

➢ I sat as a businesswoman on the first Private Industry Council for jobs in Boston. It had as one of its goals, creating jobs for the youth.

> I applied to the Sloan School of Management and would have been accepted except one female on the admissions committee informed me that if she let me in I would be teaching the class. I was refused admission.

These and many other incidents expanded me, my understanding of the world outside of my Muslim bubble. It forced me to decide what I was willing to settle for and what was my bottom line. More importantly, I took more time to think about the consequences that might come should I accept a challenge. Not every battle is a war, some are not meant to be considered. I reasoned that I had only so much stamina in my life's cup and I could not waste time dealing with skirmishes. So, I left many battlefields. I just walked away. It wasn't worth the time or energy. I am sure many saw that behavior as weak, but I assure you it was not. I was alone, no sidekick or Tonto as a backup.

Mahalia Jackson sang a song, _"Lord, don't move my mountain, just give me the strength to climb."_ I continue to ask for guidance and protection. _Thank you, Dear Holy Spirit, if I had not listened, obeyed and humbled myself, I might be dead._

The Experimental School System of Education in Massachusetts (ESSEM)

This system was originally called the Massachusetts Experimental School System. (MESS) The acronym brought forth many grins and snide remarks. Upon becoming its' executive director, I received permission to change the name to the Experimental School System of Education in Massachusetts (ESSEM)

The seventy's was fraught with the turmoil of busing. ESSEM was started by a grant of the Ford foundation to look at urban education for inner city youth from grades kindergarten to grade twelve. Ophie Franklin was its first executive director and the school was started in the Boston Museum of Science. Through a series of changes the program moved to Lena Park, on American Legion Highway, and ended up in Grove Hall, in Roxbury. Its mission and program was to bus white children into the inner city to be educated in an innovative setting, proving that desegregation could happen in Boston without violence. To my knowledge, this was the first school system in the country to be housed under a board of education.

The Metropolitan Council for Educational Opportunity (METCO) was an educational option also. It was a program that bused inner city blacks to neighboring town schools. These programs were designed to provide students academic, personal and interpersonal enrichment.

When Judge Garrity presented an order for the city of Boston to desegregate, the politics of reverse busing was a bomb waiting to explode. In 1974, I became its new executive director/superintendent, more about this later. The era of busing within Boston was violent and disturbing. The idea that busing whites into the inner city, for a quality education, with no conflict, was not viewed as an important program for state expenditures. There were always difficulties in trying to secure funding through the state legislature; other items were given a higher priority. In 1974, I became its new executive director/superintendent. While we may never be given credit for what we learned or did, this system graduated many students that moved on to become leaders in the community. When the school closed, the teaching staff moved into the Boston public school system and other local educational programs bringing their experience and talent.

This system had three schools, Lower, Middle and High. In the lower school we accepted children at four and a half years of age, which was a new idea in that day. The middle school dealt with teaching children how to read through art, music and alternate methods of the day; and the high school students had vouchers. They contracted with college professors or other professional school teachers to acquire the education they needed to graduate. This was a successful experiment. When the school closed, hired movers came to throw away all the hard work and information we had gathered. Rather than throw away the information, I took it out of the trash. I kept most of it, including the pictures; and the information.

There was a learning curve for staff as well as children. The merging of children whose parents were professionals (doctors, lawyers, etc.) with those whose parents were entrepreneurs, cleaned houses or were cooks, clerks and cab drivers, many had limited or no education. This was a factor in developing parental-peer relationships. Each person, parent and teachers alike, were stepping out of their normal comfortable group and relating through the children. Everyone learned something. Sometimes it was favorable. Other times individuals could not break through their cultural and educational leanings to relate comfortably. That takes time. We closed after three years of my administration. So this was a learning experience for all of us. There was mandatory family involvement. There were two black male principals, one in Lower school and the other in High school, and one black female middle school principal. In the Middle School, we taught English and Reading through art for those students who could hardly read, though they had been promoted to the next grade in the Boston Public School System.

We learned to acknowledge the differences in how children learn. One size does not fit all. One learning experience was the disagreement I had with the lower school principal, a Harvard graduate, who believed that when black children are ready to read they will learn. I disagreed. I believed that children with limited educational culture in the home needed to be trained. They needed to be shown how to pick up a book and read. They needed to learn how to add, subtract and multiply in their heads. More importantly they needed to view their parents and their history as important, and understand that they were following the tradition of many non-whites who wished to succeed.

They should have a goal, accept the high morals and cultural baton passed to them by their parents, and carry it forward. Many children who came to our school from the public schools recognized the lack of education of their parents, and had begun to refute much if not all that their parents had to offer. After all, weren't they being educated and weren't they smarter than their parents? Why should they have to listen to parents anymore? If their parents were not politically correct, the students were embarrassed. Everyone had television and knew how parents were supposed to act. So, we disagreed on the influence of home environment, our behavior, and its impact in a learning situation. Once again, I was still not good on politics. Our difference in perspectives became a parental confrontation from the educated and politically astute to support his educational philosophy.

He demanded to function his way and I demanded he function mine. The next thing I knew, the professional parents were demanding my resignation. After all, I only had a Master' of Education from Antioch, and he had his from Harvard, so surely he was more competent and capable than I. They called a meeting at the school and I held my ground. They went to my boss, Commissioner Anrig, and his position was "'She is the executive director, and what she says goes." That was a victory for the children. We started training the children from educationally deficient homes and began to see the benefits quickly.

It was not difficult to understand that we were dealing with many urban community parents who had experienced educational trauma. No one goes back to the scene of the crime. What do I mean by that? Many of these parents had started school, and had dropped out, for many different reasons, and school was the scene of the crime.

Some of those reasons had to do with highly educated, yet insensitive teachers who believed that their college training had given them a blueprint for success.

They were educated teachers without "mother wit,'" common sense, or moral values. Many of those teachers were unable to fathom why parents wouldn't come to school to check on their kids. I believed that the family had to be educated, and ultimately, the teachers in our school became friends and mentors. The schools were no longer a memory of past failure, with students sitting in those little seats and the "authority' figure standing in front. In that model, the students' role was to agree with everything the teacher said, even if it was contrary to their belief.

The beauty of the Experimental School is that the students of color saw their teachers at church, in the market, on the street, and just hanging out. They knew we cared. Many people felt I was too demanding of teachers and gentle with students and they were probably right. There were problems, as in any school system, but we had the support of the families, community, churches, and leaders. I did not believe we had time to play with children's lives. Education was and is a serious commitment. The responsibility to expand the minds of students through exposing them to a world of information had to be handled carefully, thoughtfully, intelligently, and not in a haphazard manner.

Just how did I become the executive director/superintendent of the system. The original head of the school had requested more money to run the school. I understood that they were bargaining. During the impasse, they decided to close the Experimental School. Again, I did not know if they would have actually done that, or not. My son was in the school and I had a vested interest in seeing it survive. They advertised the position, and I applied. I later learned that I received less than half the pay the head of the school was earning. It was not about money, it was about our children and being able to offer them a quality education.

I'm sure many will say that if no one applied for the position they would have given him what he asked. We will never know. I was running the family business, so a high salary wasn't an issue. So much learning went on in that school, yet when it closed it was as if it never existed.

Someday, we need to tell the story of the Experimental School. We need to tell the story that families matter, values are important, behavior is important, discipline matters, and that the refusal to incorporate these elements into the curriculum as a valid concern or consideration for education is a mistake. I also consider that the refusal to design challenges, at all levels, of mental and physical struggle around elements of choice, sequence and consequence, in the school system is injurious to our health as a people, a community, and a nation. The history of parents' matters, as do the errors they may have made, and what they believed or didn't believe. Thought matters, as do the reasons for the way you think. How you process information. Do you absorb everything, discern it, evaluate it, eliminate it, and why? Learning is experiential and the kind that makes a difference and lasts. Schools must be supportive of healthy home environments and show that they are, by example. The "do as I say not as I do,'" never worked and never will.

Schools, especially urban schools, should have a stricter code for hiring the kind of staff who will teach and influence children who already come from dysfunctional situations. As I write, I know you see the influence of religion or a Higher Scientific, Moral Power; home training with parents or adults being the first teachers of personal hygiene, speech, respect, decorum, morals, and love. I've said how I feel about discipline or boundaries and struggle in education. Sequence-Consequence. If students don't understand this natural law then systems should be established to require a certain acceptable standard from pre-school level on.

In nature, the smallest seed must have the right nutrients to grow. If it does not struggle through the dirt, and even cement, it cannot live and perform its mission. "'Without struggle there is no progress'" says Frederick Douglass. Remove even one of these elements listed above from the environment of children or adults, and you limit their growth and independence.

The Experimental School System in Education of Massachusetts was a success. When Judge Garrity accepted the desegregation plan of the City of Boston, the Legislature looked for money to put in the budget for busing. There was the Experimental School. We closed because of politics and finance not because of the quality of staff or program.

Picture of president Reagan

To Thelma Cromwell-Moss
With best wishes,

Ronald Reagan

The Impact of Divorce on the Business

My husbands' last act of destruction impacted how I was treated in my own community and extended into the glass business. "She did this to me, a black man. You know how those educated black woman treat us black men who do all we can but don't have an education." Well, I was part of the 8(a) small business program. The contracting officers were black males. The process was to go and identify contracts and have them approved by the contracting officer. I went and got contracts and they gave them, I was told, "'to men with families.'" I was trying to feed three children, but it didn't matter. No one wanted to help an uppity black woman.

I had participated in political parties in an effort to understand politics. Because of these efforts, I had been a guest of at least three presidents, and invited to lunch and private informational meetings at the White House. I used one of my invitations from President Reagan to share my dilemma. In desperation, I walked into the White House with a folder in my hand. I still have the picture to prove it. I explained what was happening to me. I asked him for his help. He took my folder and handed it to an aide. He said he would make a call.

Shortly after I returned from Washington, DC, the head of the Small Business Administration Office, called me for a meeting. George Allen was the head of the Boston office and a democrat. He gave me hell. Who did I think I was having someone from the White House call about me? After that, they left me alone. But still nothing was working well. I got the hard jobs, I needed help and no one here would lift a hand to help that uppity black woman. I thought I had one friend who was a community college president. He made an offer to come to Berkshire Community college, so I became a College Dean.

A College Dean

I took a position as dean of continuing education at Berkshire Community College and left the business to be run by an employee. The president wanted to develop access to women into the college. The scholarships for women were not being used, because women weren't applying. After changing the committee to include more women, surprise, a rush of women applied, and the college accepted them.

If things had run smoothly, I would have stayed. It was not meant to be. At a public affair, I was seated next to the president with his wife on the other side of him. I felt this hand on my thigh. I thought this could have been a mistake, so I moved his hand. But no, it was back. The hand continued to rub my thigh. I crushed his hand, looked him in the eye, and got up. Rage! I wanted to kill him. Once again, I was naive. I thought this was a job with no "fringe benefits.'"

The next day I told him I was resigning. There were many things that were happening, the business was failing, without my knowledge and supervision, and my children were being given special treatment that was undermining my authority. They were being considered special, and could do no wrong. They were starting to go wild. But in the end, the main reason I resigned was the president's starting of sexual abuse. I told one of the other black women on staff, and I discovered that she was aware of it. She said he liked women of color. Well, not this woman of color, ever again. Within a week I was gone. I loved that position but I would be damned if another man, white, black, blue or green would abuse me. I was out of there. *Once again, Spirit guided me and protected my family.* I later learned that the president and his wife divorced, but at least it was not because of me.

Chapter IX – Business Interest

Business Experience

I have always been interested in business. When I was seventeen, I worked in Brother Samuels' store when he had only fresh fish, chickens and greens. I cut the chickens and cleaned and filleted the fish. Seeing your efforts come alive is a very meaningful experience. I worked at the T&W restaurant with Sister Sarah and Brother Willie. I learned first hand the arduous chore of building something and the satisfaction of accomplishment. I have gone to China at least twice on business interests. On one trip I was flown North and met with the head of the Province Sheshang-shwan, (phonetic spelling) their head of environment and the finance commission. I was given a Chinese contract to sign and I refused because I couldn't read Chinese. I'm not finished yet.

By example both grandmothers encouraged me to become a contributor and participant in the world and not just a taker. Granny owned a store and rooming house and Gram'ma "Liza sewed, crocheted, knitted, did tatting and washed and ironed clothes for a living. They were both self sufficient. So it would not be unusual for me to follow in their footprints.

AA Glassmobile, Inc.

The first day I was married, my husband informed me he had lost his job with B.F. Goodrich. They had made him an offer to leave the state, he refused. From then on he held a series of jobs but not for long. He seemed to be out of work constantly, but we got by. The last time he was employed, he lost a security job and was out of work; he started working, part-time for a friend who owned a glass business. He learned how to put in windows and cut glass. He started having problems with the owner and decided that he should go on his own. In 1969 we incorporated. We purchased an old mail truck for $150 and retrofitted it to cut glass and repair windows. The children named the truck after having seen the Walt Disney picture, the Gnome mobile. They called it the Glassmobile, AA to put it in the beginning of the alphabet. I made flyers and went up and down the streets passing them out. As the business grew, I went for contracts with the housing department of the city of Boston.

I set up an appointment to meet with the manager. When I arrived he was on the phone and told me to sit. The conversation was filled with curse words and expletives; every now and then he would look up to see how I was holding up. I still believed in professional behavior, which involved no swearing. Finally, he finished his conversation and beckoned me to come to his desk. He said he was going to test me with one small contract. Our task was to be on call for broken glass at this one building, in a housing development in Dorchester. We did a good job and the next thing I knew, he was calling us for more and more work. AA Glassmobile, Inc. began to grow. In this arena, I was learning to be quiet and listen. Our business continued to expand to the point we had two or three men on the truck. Our financial status changed, I wish I could say it changed for the better. The more we got, the less we had. I couldn't understand what was happening. I was working full time, and my husband was supposed to be working full time on the truck, but we began to have less and less spending resources.

The women started coming to the house to inform me of his advances or claim his attentions. I don't know if I had a secret belief that men would always seek other women. I had certainly seen it happen in my family. One day the door bell rang and a woman with two children, one in her arms and one holding her hand was standing at the door. At that time she informed me that my husband was making advances to her. I stopped her statement in mid air and asked her to wait there. I marched upstairs and told my husband someone wanted him at the door. I don't know the discussion between them. She left and he came back upstairs. My statement to him was, "Don't ever bring that stuff to this house again." That was it. He seemed to down alcohol by the case; and engaged in drinking sprees when I wasn't home. Then suddenly, he felt compelled to move to a one family house. We moved six blocks away, but he thought he had moved to nirvana. I wanted house help and private schools for my children; he seemed to want more alcohol, marijuana and smokes. My escape was working as the educator and business woman, 24/7.

Again, Spirit guided me to take notice of where I was: the present. After the divorce and I returned from my deanship I immersed myself in glazing contracting. I began to look at bigger jobs.

Corona Architectural Glazing

All the work that I was aware of in the government was union controlled. If I wanted to work on those contracts, I needed a union house. Corona Architectural Glazing was the company I created to do union work. In the trade you would have considered me 'double breasted' because I had a union and non-union house.

We got a job to install mirrors at the Harvard Business School dormitory. The union called and asked if they could send over a worker who was older. Since you do favors to get favors, I said okay. The person he did send could not carry the mirrors up the steps, or do any of the work required. I called the union steward and told him that this man could not perform the task. The response was, "'Have your sons carry the glass up the stairs, and hold it in place while he puts the screws in." Rage, and flashbacks, struck me. Once again a white man was being paid for non-performance while my sons were doing all the work. My sons were hardly taking home a salary, and they were not allowed to be in the union. In my opinion that was racist. That was slavery, and I was not going to put my sons in that situation. I shut the job down, and opened it up as a non-union job. I got a lot of flack, and met with the head of the Harvard Property Division, who listened to me and allowed me to finish the job, which turned out to be a success.

I received a contract to put the first two floors of glazing, glass windows and doors in the Thomas P. 'Tip" O'Neill Federal Building. I believe this was arranged by

Divine permission. This was an unexpected opportunity. The Dimeo Bros. Construction Company out of Rhode Island did not know me, but they took a chance on me. They called me to their offices and suggested that if I ran into any trouble to contact them. I believed I was on my way. Just do a good job, I told myself, and you will be able to employ others and create a decent living for yourself and family. I remember going to meetings with all the contractors. There were times I would raise my hand to speak and was always ignored. Finally one of the older men in the room came to me and told me if I wanted to be acknowledged, I would have to speak louder and maybe swear. I ignored his suggestion until I got tired of being ignored. The next time I raised my hand and the head person perused the room intending to ignore me, I spoke up. "Damn it, I have something to say." From then on when his eyes perused the room to consider comments, he made sure to call on me. At times he would ask me specifically if I had a comment. From then on I learned that certain language was appropriate, given the situation, to secure the necessary attention. I was no longer the seemingly sweet woman.

It was a great opportunity, or so I thought. I tried working with the glaziers union. I wanted my sons in the union. My sons could join the union, but they couldn't work on any of my jobs or in Boston. I was told that it was a rule of the union. That was unacceptable.

I was the only black female with a glazing company in Massachusetts and maybe in the country. The glaziers union people and I were constantly battling about who would have control of my company. They told me, "You go get the work, and we'll run the company.'" I had just lived through sixteen years of a man living vicariously through my efforts, so I was not about to turn over this company to a man or a union. Maybe I misunderstood, it happens, but at the time the words meant what was said: if I gave the iron-workers their share of the work, I was caught between them and the glaziers. If I gave the carpenters a share of the work, I was caught between them and the glaziers. It became so constant that I contacted the AFL-CIO in New York. They sent people down to mediate our differences, but they would agree with me and the glaziers union would continue to make my life difficult.

One day a new pallet of glass arrived for installation at the site; it was set off in a corner of the building in no one's way, but it mysteriously 'crashed.' The pallet was totally destroyed. Because of that, I was cited by the head of construction for holding up the job because they had to have the windows in so the interior work could begin. I went to my trailer and cried. It was pay day. The workers came in and saw my red eyes. A few of them started laughing, and one said, "Look at her crying, the black bitch." Rage, just outright rage, came to me as I handed him his check. All the teachings of the white man, as the devil arose. Back came all the memories of sitting in the back of the bus, drinking from colored only fountains, and going to colored only toilets or using out houses and grass when nothing else was available. All the hardship in my life came flooding back, and now this white man was standing here accepting my check for twenty-one dollars an hour and calling me a black bitch.

I got through the payroll and went home. Furious. I told my son who was about nineteen at the time. The next day he went down to the job site and wanted to see that son-of-a-bitch who had called his mother a black bitch. My son was going to throw his ass off the building. For the next few days, my son came with me to the job. They either hustled the man out, or he didn't show.

That Friday and Saturday evening I heard all this pounding and banging in the street outside my door. There was a red truck with men in the back with bats pounding and screaming."We know where you live."' I wasn't scared, I was angry. I decided that if that was the way they wanted to play, I would put a hit out on them. I didn't know anybody, but I put the word out.

Then I had a meeting with a fellow contractor, a plumber. He sat me down and explained to me that he had gone to prison because he had killed someone for pouring cement down his work and messing up his life and company. He looked at me hard, 'Thelma, think of what you're doing. You have three children to raise. Who will take care of them when you're gone? They don't want their mother in jail.' Once again, Spirit stepped in, and I had to take a long hard look at what I was becoming. I had to face the rage, the hate, the anger, and what was really happening to me. Spiritual consciousness stepped in. What was I becoming and was I happy? I thought about it a long time.

Thank you, Dear Holy Spirit for sending this angel in human form to force me to reconsider what path I was taking.

In the end, I decided to close the union house. I met with the steward of the glaziers union. Once again he informed me to go get the work and he would run my business. I said no. If I had to pay the piper, then I would call the tune. He told me that there was five million dollars worth of glazing work in the pipe line coming to me. He told me that only a fool would walk away from five million dollars. I guess I was the fool. I called the prime contractors, Dimeo Bros. of Rhode Island, and told them I was turning back the contracts that were not started. They asked me if I wanted to sell them. I said no. I was tired, and I was leaving the field. I had been beaten up enough, and my children's lives were at stake. My family had been threatened and like a mother lion, I was ready for the kill. I saw nobody coming to my aid. I decided to leave now before I killed somebody, or my children were injured.

I talked to several of my friends and told them I was leaving town. They tried to encourage me to stay. I was blinded by fury. One more day in this town, seeing the smiling faces, facing the lies and deception, was one day too many. I was bloodied and they had bent me; and I needed time to heal. I left Boston and moved to Maryland.

Being A Change Agent

My niece by marriage had lost her job in the airlines. I thought that I could help her get back on her feet by living with her. This had been her first job and she kept it for twenty-five years, so when she lost it, she was devastated. I went and got a job at Kelly Girls' for six dollars per hour. She chided me for taking a job with menial pay, with all my 'education.' I explained to her that this was temporary, a means to an end, and that she should try it. "'I'll never be a secretary," was her reply. "What will you do when unemployment runs out?" I asked. "'Don't worry. I'll be back to work by then or have a better job."

Quickly I became a Kelly Girls' secretary on demand who was paid twelve to thirteen dollars per hour for being on call. She couldn't see the value of what I was doing. She ended up going back to California with her parents. I learned from this experience that with all I knew or thought I could do by example, I could not help or assist a change in her perception or values. She first had to become aware of her present state, the *it is*; then she would have to want to change; then and only then would my efforts make sense to her. I stayed in Maryland eleven years, long enough to become an elected official in the Republican Party along with Michael Steele. My daughter was in Military School in Virginia at the time. She graduated from Potomac High in Maryland, and later went to Washington College. Now there are some stories.

My Trip to Africa

Every one should visit Africa. I really do mean everyone. The learning experience is phenomenal. Malcolm used to remind me to travel. "The world will never be the same once you travel", and so I traveled to Japan, China, the Caribbean, Mexico and Africa.

As much as I would have liked to go to Africa, it was not the item on my agenda when Brother Frederick came to my house at 62 Richfield Street, Dorchester, Massachusetts. He was the entrepreneur of the Muslim community, and someone to emulate. We were both not participating in the Ummah (Mosque) at Intervale Street. He asked me to come outside. We talked at his car. He explained that he was working with a brother in Africa and needed me to verify the transfer of money. I was to receive ten percent of the total money to help me with my business. He explained that he could not go because of his business interests, and since I was not working then he would pay my expenses to take his place. Well, I thought, what could be a better chance to further my business and enjoy a free trip? I was naïve, I did not realize that it was a scam, and without knowing all the particulars, I took the trip, and financing. I was intent on helping a brother. I dare not tell my children because they would have said, emphatically, no.

So, I planned my trip to Africa, Abidjan in Côte d'Ivoire. Brother Frederick gave me money for the trip and extra cash for hotel and expenses. But, Divine Spirit, or God, continues to look out for babies and fools. We got off the plane in Senegal, and we did a circular pass through the building. The authorities checked our passports and if we wanted to purchase something from the local culture, we could have. Upon entry in the building, I saw men in fatigues with machine guns. They were laughing and pumping their arms as they raised their machine guns up and down.

I went up to the man in charge and asked him what this was all about. Were we in danger? Why was it that the first thing I saw in my Mother Land were men with machine guns? What was going on here? His demeanor changed and softened. Oh no, he assured me. He went over to the men sitting around smoking, laughing and brandishing their guns and the next thing I knew they were gone behind the curtain.

Then, this same gentleman, took me over the runways to a fence and told me to lean over. "That is where your mothers and fathers were brought and put on slave ships to be taken to the United States." We talked about history and the experiences of children of slaves returning to Africa. He was intelligent, wise and very comforting. I apologize here for not remembering his name, but he really made me feel at home, as if I were family. Situations happen to teach us.

Thank you Dear Holy Spirit for putting him in my path.

We boarded the plane and went on to Côte d'Ivoire. When I stepped off the plane, something warm and comforting welcomed me, something holy and special. I kneeled and thanked the Creator for allowing me to return home. I felt like something or someone had thrown a warm blanket of love and protection around me. As I write about this experience, I can still feel what it was like.

I was met at the airport by two men who informed me they were taking me to a hotel in the bush. I let them know that I had already booked a hotel room in the city, but they let me know that these arrangements were made because of the secrecy of this situation. Warning signs started pelting my head but I went anyway. We arrived at the hotel in the bush.

The manager was a very nice looking woman who looked like so many African Americans. She was thin, had black hair straightened, and was pleasant. She seemed a little surprised at her new hotel guest. I asked her if she had a fax machine. She did. I sent a fax to my children informing them that I was in Africa, I was staying at this hotel, and that I wanted them to send me a return fax to confirm that they received mine.

My red warning signs were becoming stronger and stronger. I was led into a room that was clean and neat, and it even had a television. However, the door looked as if it had been put back together after having been bashed into splinters. I did a pirouette and sat on the bed and turned on the television, concerned. Now my head was pounding and my stomach was queasy. A squirrel or a moth or anyone could have come through that door, just by pushing gently. I didn't have a gun, knife, brick or my mother's baseball bat.

Time to go! I called downstairs and told the owner to call me a cab. She told me that the room had been paid for a week and didn't I want to stay one night. But I told her I had made previous arrangements and wanted her to call a cab for me. While in front of her, I contacted the hotel where I had already made a reservation, and I indicated to the one on the phone where I was and that a cab would be bringing me to the hotel. She called the cab. I left after informing her to please tell the men to contact me where I would be staying.

As I look back, I recall that I never broke a sweat. Divine Spirit as usual was with me. My voice was calm, controlled, and authoritative. I arrived at my hotel to await the arrival of the "African' whom I was to meet to confirm the financial arrangements. I faxed my children letting them know that I had changed hotels and gave them the new fax number.

The next day around 11:00 a.m., a young man with beautiful diamond rings on eight of his fingers came to see me. His rings were an ostentatious display of wealth. He had a beautiful smile and tried to exhibit the English decorum for this "unusual lady," which was one of his names for me. I was Madame Moss or Lady Thelma. He left and planned to return around 2:00 p.m. in the afternoon, and take me to the "African" whom Brother Frederick had been dealing with. He came at that time, and we went.

We arrived at a house that reminded me of the houses in the Caribbean, that were painted pink and expansive. I was brought into the house and introduced to the 'African.' I don't remember his name. He wasn't what I had expected; he was not dark in color but about my complexion. I was ushered into a living room, where I guess we were to have small talk. At this point, there was nothing that I wanted to have small talk about. I was here to find the money, get my money, and get out of Africa alive. Then he took me into a room where three pink cases were on the floor, and a man was sniffing and coughing and acting as their guardian. They measured three feet by five feet by three feet. The top and front of one of the cases was open. I saw piles of one hundred dollar bills stacked from top to bottom, front to back, $100,000 per pack.

Without a change of facial expression, I asked, "Now what?" The 'African' then informed me that he needed four hundred dollars to pay for one of these cases to be shipped to the United States. Of course, I said, "No problem. Just use the money in those cases to pay for all the expenses." All the while the guardian of these cases was sneezing, wheezing and coughing into what was once a white handkerchief, which was turning brown from lack of washing.

I asked the question, "'Why can't you use this money to pay the expenses needed to move this money?'" "Well,'" he said, 'We need to have a show of good faith from our brother in America. There are people to pay off, and other costs that we might not foresee, so that we can safely move this money.'" Again, I displayed no facial expression, but my mind was moving, checking, questioning, answering, and debating. 'Why would we have to come up with money? Why couldn't he just use the money, or was it counterfeit? Were we being expected to give good money for counterfeit? Even if it was not counterfeit, why did he need to have an American partner when he could have paid off people in his government, gotten a passport gone to an off-shore island or Lichtenstein, put it in a bank and none would be the wiser?

Why is the rich African looking for help from the poor American?' Well, after confirming that there were three cases of United States hundred dollar bills, we went back to the living room.

He talked of Dr. Martin Luther King, Jr. and Malcolm X and their belief to see black Americans become a part of the international retail and industrial market. He very quickly insisted that he must send this money to help his brother in America. I again asked why he couldn't use this money here. I didn't receive an intelligent answer. Then I said that I needed to think about his proposition and would later get back to him. I really needed to get back to the hotel, out of this environment and in safe territory. As I was leaving, I turned to him and said, "Do me a favor. Take some of that money and take that guardian to a hospital, he needs medical help." I got in the car and left. We arrived at the hotel and I told the young man with the rings that I would call him tomorrow with my decision.

Of course, when I called, I informed them that there would be no money coming from the United States and that I had informed Brother Frederick. Of course, I still had not talked to Brother Frederick because I was wondering what kind of brother would put me in this situation. Well, I had six more days of staying in Africa.

I went to an American Express office to verify details about my return trip home. There was a young black African girl sitting with an Afrikan, a white African. In his need to impress the ticket person, and me, he was rubbing the girls' breasts and pulling her clothes off and talking sexually to her. She was embarrassed and tried to get him to stop. Then he told her and anyone who could hear, how he owned her body and soul as well as her pickaninnies. She looked at me wanting to die. I nodded to her. As our eyes met, I acknowledged that I saw no shame on her. It drew me back to what it must have been like during slavery in America, when women tolerated every indecency to protect their children and save their lives. I was half way around the world and yet no one in the room or the area felt compelled to call 911. Here in the Motherland this public mauling of a woman was acceptable. I felt very sad for her. I felt powerless to help.

I went to the local university and met several professors. I walked around the city and got a sense of the area. I met students and made a life long friend and brother in Yaya Ouattara. He has since married and finished college. He is my connection to the Motherland. He introduced me to African music, dance and his history. His parents and family are Kings and Queens in the Motherland, and they still own land.

I thank you Holy Spirit for Malcolm, Martin Luther King, Brother Frederick, YaYa, the military head in Senegal, and the remembrance of people you brought in my path because of this journey. I thank you dear Creator God for your Divine guidance, protection and arrangements.

I arrived home, safe and sound. Brother Frederick came by to see me. He never asked me about the trip but said he was glad to see I had returned home safe. Maybe three or four months later, he stopped by and with tears in his eyes, he broke down and cried. He told me he hadn't the courage to go himself. He thought it might be dangerous, but he had prayed for me all the time. I thanked him for asking me and trusting me to represent him.

My Spiritual Guides and God are Awesome. Thank you, Dear Holy Spirit for never leaving my side.

AAG Industries, Inc. (An Act of God)

In 1987 I was working at an environmental law firm in the Washington, DC area. A lawyer returned from court telling me he was going out to get drunk. When I asked why, he informed me that he had won the case for his client but the children had lost. It seems that the case had to do with polluted water coming up on the playground and the children having afflictions. I promised the Creator if ever I could do something about cleaning up polluted water, I would.

That Sunday while reading the newspaper I found that a group of twenty-one International Scientists were meeting in Washington, DC. I checked out the conference, found a list of the scientists and institutions they represented, researched their addresses and sent letters to them requesting any new technology they might have had on cleaning water. As I look back, only a Divine Arrangement could have given me this scenario. Out of the twenty-one, I narrowed it down to twelve and after much consideration I settled on a Turkish scientist, Niyazi Bicak. I agreed to bring him over to the United States. We signed agreements on his percentage and participation to help develop the water cleaning chemicals he had researched. I had gone to Suffolk Law School but did not finish. However, I had learned enough to find a polymer scientist with legal experience, who helped me file for a patent and become successful in securing a patent in November, 2000.

Wanting to follow through on my business-political training, I went to the state government to ask for assistance and test my polymer. I was excited. A meeting was called, and I met with polymer scientists from the University of Amherst. They informed me that they would test my polymer, sample and have an answer for me within two to four weeks. Well, the weeks turned into months and I kept calling the state office about a report. I never received one. The University of Massachusetts-Amherst polymer division ignored my letters, and calls and, to date has all my information; but never responded to me.

About six months later, Siemens AG, a German multinational company heralded a unique exchange polymer, the newest technique in the cleaning of water. Most of the words were taken directly from my proposal, even down to the 'T" bag. I had not protected my patent overseas and now it was gone. The state and the University of Amherst polymer division acknowledged receipt of my information but never helped me. I had lost a possibility and an opportunity or better yet, my ideas had been stolen and I would never receive credit for my work or efforts. I still have the letter that says they would help me.

Later, I made a presentation at the MIT Enterprise Forum. I took my daughter. I was informed that my patent and water cleaning technology was like the beginning of the computer age. There was sufficient belief in my technology that I was invited to a Venture Capital affair at Arthur D. Little a major research company in Cambridge. There was a buzz, where is she, there she is. I ended up with a circle of people discussing my technology and finally the bomb shell was dropped. "We'll take 80 percent of your idea and help you." Well, I think they thought I was sophisticated, and understood the rules. I did not.

Before I could regain my presence of mind and recoup my training as a professional, I blurted out, "'look if I'm going to be raped, I want to enjoy it." I said the wrong thing to the right people. From then on, my life as a boot strapping entrepreneur became just that. Help came from no where. I met one venture capitalist through the Center for Women Entrepreneurs (CWE) and I asked, 'If I give you 80 percent of my company will you agree to...'" and he cut me off and replied, "'If I own 80 percent of your company, I don't have to agree to anything."

A consultant accountant of CWE informed me that I should sell the patent because I didn't have a PhD in science or manufacturing, and knew nothing about the chemical industry, and couldn't make it in that industrial world. I went home that night and thought long and hard. He's right! I know management, and have taught business courses. I've initiated ideas and brought them to fruition, but I'd worked on things I knew, and, at least had a good working knowledge of the arenas that I worked in. Now, I was asking someone to do for me what I was not willing to do for myself, step back and learn. So I went back to school.

During all this time I had spent my money bringing the scientist, Mr. Bicak, back and forth to the United States. I paid a minimum of three times to register him and support him for his scientific conferences and meetings. I paid him as a consultant, in the belief that he would live up to his bargain. In 2006, I negotiated a part-time teaching position for him at a Middlesex Community College. He was to stay for a semester and work part-time with me to get the business off the ground. Well, then the problems began. The president, Carole Cowan, was a female, the head of sciences was a female, and every position that he was concerned about was headed by a woman. I had never imagined that his cultural leanings could be a problem at the school.

Finally, I asked him to call friends and advisors of mine who were working at Johnson & Johnson. I gave him a phone card. He then informed me that if they wanted to talk to him they were to call him or come to see him. Apparently, he was an important man in his country and did not have to account to women or make phone calls to companies. By this time, I had really learned to listen to him. He wanted me to give him my contacts, but clearly he had no intention of helping me. I was being used, again. Within one week, he was back on a plane to Turkey. When he left he told me that he wanted nothing to do with the patent, and he was doing new research. It didn't matter. He had not kept his agreement to assist in the development of the technology, nor was he willing to 'talk with women' who might be his superiors in responsibilities. I was crushed.

So, given these scenarios I signed up for classes in biotechnology at Middlesex Community College. I was broke by then, and I looked for financial help and scholarships, but ended up once again filing for student loans. Well, I said I needed to learn. I said I wanted to know this arena, and now I had to prove to myself that my course compass headings were correct. I could come out of this educational phase combining my new found knowledge of science with my years of experience in small business, manufacturing, training in polymers and manufacturing from Wisconsin University.

I will finish school in December and be awarded an Associate Degree in Biotechnology dated January 2011, by Divine Permission. The patent has ten more years to go. I need to have lab and financial assistance to make my dream a reality. Unlike the founders of this country, I can't (nor would I) use slaves to make this dream a reality. The rules and laws of the time demand substantial financing to be a part of the pharmaceutical and water industries.

So, I write. I need to develop a team that is willing to follow the dream of its dreamer to fruition. I need a group that thinks globally, is not uncomfortable with working with a female who recognizes her imperfection, and is open. It is my intent to publish my memoirs and raise enough money to complete the dream.

Chapter X – IT IS

Return to Boston

My mother's cancer brought my daughter and me back to Boston in December of 1992. She had been ill for a long time but I never knew it. When she had deteriorated to the point she was hospitalized, she told my brothers to contact me because I could do something. She died in 1993. My father had a stroke. I went to the hospital to see him. He had a difficult time recovering. Later, he ended up in a nursing home. I visited him and was horrified by the situation he was in. Here was my dad in a dark blue painted room with three other men. He was in a high chair with a diaper on and unable to feed himself. He cried and so did I. I fed him. I called my sister and she was able to put him in a brand new facility that had just opened. I remember my Gram'ma 'Liza's words, and they had come to pass. I kept my promise. He passed in 1996. In either case I thought I could have made their lives easier if I had only known what was going on by offering them Divine Light. It didn't matter. I would have plenty of time to put more guilt on myself, more pain at not having been the "savior" of those I loved. Who died and left me God? What made me think that I could change the consequences in people's lives, consequences that they had set in motion years ago? I have prayed for their souls and ask that they sit in warm breezes, beside cool waters, and enjoy the time they have in their after-life. I have a broader understanding of Qur'an and

Islam, the Universe and the One Creator God because of my journey. Along the way I met a group named Sukyo Mahikari out of Japan.

Sukyo Mahikari

Like many groups that have begun with a message, the word 'cult' comes to mind. Most groups that start to offer a different reference point of thought are placed in that category. So is Sukyo Mahikari.

Like Christianity and the Nation of Islam, in my experience, it will get rave reviews and condemnation. Fear of the unknown and the possibility of change will be a factor in making a decision to experience the Universal Light. I am thankful to the Honorable Elijah Muhammad and all my teachers and mentors who constantly reminded me to search and question, knowing that my Spiritual Guardians would not lead me astray. Information and experiential learning allows me to grow.

All my life I had 'so-called' mysterious things happen to me. They included the Light at the foot of my bed, or the voices in my head, or the cries from the cemetery. If people had known, they would have put me in a rubber room. I never mentioned the things that happened because I thought I was crazy at times. In 1992, my former sister-in-law and I were walking through the 7th Street open market of Washington DC. Someone put a flyer in my hand, asking me to experience the Light. My former sister-in-law, Edith, suggested we continue to walk by, but I figured if anything crazy were to happen I was in a public market, so how threatening could that be? I received the Light to my Third Eye or my Main Soul for ten minutes. Then they gave me Light on my back.

I felt at peace but it was no big thing. I left. The next day I was driving near the memorials of the war heroes, and it dawned on me that there were no cries of the dead. I stopped, circled, and drove past again, no cries. I always heard cries from cemeteries and war memorials which is why I stayed away from them. The only thing I could attribute it to was the Light. I went back to the market and got more Light. They told me they had a center on Connecticut Avenue. I decided to go.

I was apprehensive because this could turn out to be another religion, a cult and jive organization. I had had it with both, I knew the spin. But remarkably, this seemed different. The people there offered to teach me how to give the Light. If I took a Primary Course for one weekend, Friday, Saturday and Sunday, I could become a giver of Light. Of course I had to pay for the course, but I couldn't charge anyone to whom I gave Light. This was a new twist. The Light was offered to remove toxins and allow the body to heal itself which is its' original design.

I signed up. It is a practice, not a religion. If what they say is true, then it is not in competition with any of the present religious tenets. I could raise my hand like the prophets and sages of old, and by Divine Permission things would happen. There would be subtle changes initially and then notice-able changes, that seemed to eliminate physical toxins, stress and give me peace. As the layers of the onion of negativity peeled away, situations changed, and each time I felt closer to the Creator God, The Universe, and Divine Spiritual Consciousness. The infinitesimal particles of energy, what many are calling the quantum particles flowing through me were enhancing and enriching my thought process.

In 2006 my daughter sent me to Ohio to help her father because there was the possibility of his toe being removed, because it was turning black, a response to his diabetes. This was the final chapter for me in spiritual training of letting go and letting God. I went to his house. I offered what I had come to know was Universal Light of the Creator God. It removed toxins and allowed the body to heal which was its original design. I spent a week offering him Divine Light and the blackness on the toe reduced. I gave him Light to his main soul through his Third Eye. I was surprised he was willing to accept my offer. On the day I left he asked me to give him more of the Light, and I did. I left him telephone numbers of people in the area willing to come and offer him Light, since there is no charge. He never called.

It is now 2012, after returning to his habits of drinking and smoking, he lies in ICU. I have been to Ohio offering him this Universal Light and each time his body has responded in a positive manner, however, his body has been tortured by his life style that even our prayers and the offering of Light might not be sufficient. The Creator God will make the final decision. I write this in my memoirs because I have been allowed to assist him, pray for him and call on the Creator to have mercy and compassion while he suffers this ordeal. Someone asked me if I feel any anger: Not one iota. I was at peace in my soul with our relationship long ago. I know the God Consciousness in him is there. I ask that the Source that is not created but creates, known by many names as Jesus, Allah, Jehovah, and Su God will hear my prayers to comfort his children while they go through this challenge and grant their father mercy, and compassion.

Thank you, dear Parent God, for assisting me through these trials and allowing me to let go and let God. As I continue this journey, guide me.

I have offered Light to many persons and none have been negatively impacted, to my knowledge. It aides in the removal of toxins; so far in my experience, it works. Given my experience, I would suggest and encourage the readers to investigate Sukyo Mahikari. If it is 'sweet on your tongue and warms your heart' learn it, and use it. I also caution any that consider learning this practice not to make it more than it is. It is informational, therapeutic and spiritual, and aids in the removal of toxins. It is not a religion. Your belief system is not required for it to work. Like the sun, it is. I believe it is a gift from the Creator God in this day and time for anyone regardless of wealth, education, political status, age, ethnicity, national origin, or color. Again, it is not another religion.

In my opinion, the Christians, Muslims, Taoists and Jews have chronicled the necessary guidelines of moral conduct. Do not get caught up in the side bars that can entrap you, and discourage you from experiencing the Light energy. More importantly, let us feel free to diligently investigate any opportunity and all possibilities that will bring us closer to our Creator God and help humankind. Do not become caught up in 'leaders,' in any group or religion. This is your journey; go direct to the Source of Creation, God, by any name you choose. God knows the true believers and is no respecter of persons. I believe since we are all praying to One God, being upright and following the example of the Anointed Ones which include Abraham-Moses, Jesus and Muhammad (PBUH and all the anointed Ones) that nothing should be able to sway us from the Lighted path, one way or another. Seek, and ye shall find; knock and the door shall be opened.

Now because of my experience with the Light and all of my religious pursuits, I have developed a term that I can relate to. Now I feel I have become a M.U.T.T, a *Multi-ethnic, Ultimate, Thinking, Threat.*

My personal thoughts and what I think I learned

Right now these are my beliefs; before I pass, they might change.

> ➤ All of the Islamic, Hebrew, Christian, Buddhist and Taoist teachings converge on a Universal level of Spiritual Consciousness for me.

> ➤ There should be no compulsion in any religion, but certainly guidelines, to be grateful and thankful for everything; do no harm.

> ➤ There is One Creator God in charge. The good, the bad and the ugly eventually show that it is all related to good.

This was my journey on the lighted path of the road less traveled and my awareness of the Christ and God Consciousness in me.

It would be easy to blame someone for the twists and turns of my life. I take full responsibility before human beings and God. As I write this chronicle of my journey and through studies of Christianity, Islam, Judaism, Buddhism, Taoism and anointed writings, I speak the message that makes my everything. "*Thank you God for everything.*" I've become less accepting of structured religions. Human beings seem to step in and embellish the MESSAGE of the Anointed Ones. They try to make it more understandable and in doing so insert their view or meaning. Like Gram'ma 'Liza asked, "Do you believe in One God, One Divine Spirit, One Creator, One Source?" I do. "Will you love your fellow human being as you love yourself?"

But first, love yourself, and get to know yourself, eliminate the negativity that we carry or espouse. Move closer to the center of your God consciousness and let's make the world a better place. I continue to learn who I am and my mission for coming. This becomes my prayer, to remember, I am Spirit in a physical body, on an earthly journey.

When you go on a journey, you should have some growth, new perspectives, information to share, maybe even change. I know that:

> ➤ All Spiritual, inspired teachings and tenets come from ONE God. This One Source is not created but the source of All Creation. I have read the major religious books and there is a familiar theme vibrating within them all. I found it, now you go find it. Read!

➢ All religions will return to acknowledge their Creator God;

➢ Many religions speak of a Day of Judgment. A Day when we will be judged on our choices. Be careful how you choose.

➢ What ever you believe, Do No Harm.

➢ Love nature and your fellow human beings.

➢ You must learn to love yourself, first. Peel the negativity that keeps you from being close to the Creator God.

➢ When you help humanity, that is serving God. You decide what that means for you.

➢ We should be the best example as a Christian, Muslim, Buddhist, Taoist or human being.

➢ Money might make the journey comfortable but it will not replace good health, sound mind, or love.

➢ It is your choice and your consequence; there is no substitute or stand-in for you on that Day of Reckoning & Accounting.

My mistakes

This life has been a journey of love, laughter, pain and suffering. Much of the pain and suffering I had because I chose not to let go of the experience and forgive myself and others. Sometimes I choked on life because I was weak and the anger of yesterday filled my today. I suffered because I wanted and chose to remember the pain.

Sometimes I wallowed in it because I felt I was, **right**, as if being right is/was important. Being right is being stiff, you break; being flexible you can live for another day to learn more. *Things change. All Things Change, all the time. New information changes how we think and do.* That is a natural law of God and the Universe. Therefore one must be mindful of the day, the time and the seasons.

I believed much wrong was done to me and I let it rule my life. I missed the dance. Well I almost missed the dance. By learning to accept rejection and pain as a part of living and seeking balance in all things, I have grown and begun to heal. There are no accidents in the Universe. It took a long time, but I am thankful I became aware on *This Lighted Path, The Road Less Traveled.* May your awareness come early in your journey.

It is a new beginning for me. For everything there is a time, a purpose and a season.

This is my time to enjoy the dance.

Picture of Mother,

Debts of Gratitude I owe to those who crossed my path.

This process of memoirs and possible playwright is dedicated to my grandmother Eliza Jane McCotter (McCarter), a Native American who was my first teacher, love and mentor. With a third grade education she gave me the foundation that I needed for my Spiritual Journey by telling me, "You are an Old Soul. Do you believe in One God?" I later learned how profound those statements are and what she meant. She is an example for all so-called oppressed because she never allowed the problems of the world to enter her Spiritual Space and change who she was.

There are no accidents in the Universe, humans are not owners of the earth but responsible and accountable to the Creator God for the care and protection of the earth. We can not be proud of our stewardship.

When I have a song-poem performance in the future it is dedicated to my mother Al Hajja Amatullah Sabreen Shakir. [named Ahchi, her native American name] I thought she was the harshest trainer in my life. However, were it not for her, I could not have survived my most grueling experiences and moved on. She trained me by saying, "'What are you crying for, get up, get up. You don't have no time to cry. Keep it moving." *Thank you Dear Creator God for allowing me to be her daughter and to learn how to survive in a most unique journey.*

This Spiritual Journey writing I again dedicate to my children, Willie J, Marwan J, and Namala T, who travelled with me through much of the anguish I have experienced and never lost faith in me. I have never lost faith in them, and may their journeys be uplifting and less tragic than mine. God grant them the strength, power, discernment, love and guidance to have a life full of good health, harmony and prosperity. (ken, wa, fu)

To Kendra al-Kaleem, Robert Redd, Qasim Abdul-Tawaab and Sheryl Renee Dailey, thank you for your support, fellowship, insight and friendship. My prayer is that all your wishes, wants and needs will be granted and you will enjoy your journey.

To the following names and others I might have failed to mention who were my teachers, trainers and whetstones that polished me, aiding me in the process, I thank you. Because of you I still love the Creator God and acknowledge the Divine Spiritual influence as I move closer to my physical journeys' end.

Tony Bennett, the singer, Mr. Long, my public speaking teacher and friend, El Hajj Malik Shabazz, Malcolm X, Dr. Martin Luther King, Dean Howard Thurman, Reverend Fisher, Elijah and Clara Muhammad, Imam Warith Deen Muhammad, Mr. Louis Farrakhan (Louis X) George F. Beasley, Brother Willie and Sarah Harris, Brother Frederick, Albie (Tracey) Edwards, Wayne Budd, Ruth Batson, Senator Edward Kennedy, for the First Small Business Congress This led me to create, Women in National & International Business (an organization I established), Dr Carole Cowan, president of Middlesex Community College, President Carter, President Reagan, Eleanor Strapp, director of the Boston YWCA, her assistant Evelyn, Dorothy Height, Virginia Ehrlich, Mrs. Bleckley, Mrs. Jackson who minded the children at the church when we had the first program of the YWCA, Atty. Glendora Putman, Helen Davis, mortician, Ruby Jackson, Grace Diggs, Joyce King, Ms Melia of the ASA Gray School, the head of the boys at Milton Academy and the head of the Athletics Department in 1973, the Catholic Church, Cardinal Cushing, Tremont Temple Church and Aunt Margaret and Mama Dear, Park Street Church, AME Zion on Columbus Ave., Reverend Brown, St. Cyprian's Episcopal Church on Tremont Street, Darnley Corbin, Willie Moss, Sr., Sukunishisama, Oshinushisama, Seishinushisama, Sukyo Mahikari, William Roberts of Sukyo Mahikari, Gram'ma Liza, an Arapahoe or Cherokee Native American (but I'm still not sure because they say she came from the North); Gram'ma Rose, a Lumpi Native American; Uncle Richard, Fred (killed when I was twelve years old, he was fourteen, for not getting off the sidewalk when a white woman walked by in downtown New Bern, NC); Gregory Anrig, Commissioner of the Department of Education; Purchase of 35 Intervale St; In the performance of ORGENA, played Sister Sylvia, Cousin Edna, George Walter Cromwell Sr. and Abdul Kareem (Anthony Leo Cromwell) Shakir, John Cromwell, Robert Cromwell, my brothers; my sister Vivian Cromwell, her mother, Frances W. Cromwell and the Shepard family; AFL-CIO, carpenters union, iron workers, glaziers union, Harvard Business School (glass installation)and the head property manager at Harvard University (at the time); the Tip O'Neill Bldg builders; 8a Program and managers of the program; Black Presidents of New England, Contractors Association of Boston, I am a former president.

Books I read during my journey.

> ➤ The Bible, authorized King James version

> ➤ The Teaching of Buddha, Bukkyo Dendo Kyokai translation, copyright 1966

➢ The Message of the Qur'an, Muhammad Asad, translated and explained, copy right 1980, 1984

➢ Life & Teachings of the Masters of the Far East, Baird T. Spalding, copyright 1955

➢ The Art of War – and the Lost Art of War , Thomas Cleary, translated with commentary, copyright 1996

➢ The Taoist Classics, Thomas Cleary, translator, copyright 1990, 1991, 1994

➢ The Tao Te Ching, Stephen Mitchell, copyright 1988

➢ The Tao of Personal Leadership, Diane Dreher, copyright 1996

➢ The Tao of Leadership, John Heider, copyright 1985

➢ The Prophet, Khalil Gibran, 1923, 1986

.... **Phase Two**

Before I leave this side, I would like to share:

- ➤ My Lighted Path – *my life and other writings*; Thelma@ my-lighted-path.com

- ➤ An evening with Thelma – *a performance of music, my songs and poems;* Thelma@my-lighted-path.com

and impact:

- ➤ AAG Research Institute – *ideas I have been given in science;* masad@aagresearchinstitute.com

- ➤ AAG Industries, Inc. – *the manufacturing arm of my ideas;* aagindustries@aol.com

- ➤ S and C Academy – *Sequence/Consequence, an educational design I believe works;* awareness@sequence-con-sequence academy.com

- ➤ TCMoss Consulting – *An opportunity to consult in ways that will be of benefit;* Thelma@tcmoss consulting.com

All of these will be housed in AAG Foundation, Inc., a 501c(3), non-profit corporation except the manufacturing arm, AAG Industries, Inc.

Finally, I would like to see a facility housing an area of '**Light Giving**,' as expressed by Sukinushisama, the first Light Giver of Sukyo Mahikari of Japan; a restaurant of **healthy eating**, a **FAB LAB (of MIT)** *openly designed for 'whosoever will'* and an **educational center** which would house *a teacher training unit and a pilot school* and any other beneficial offer, physical or mental, that assists humankind on their journey to their 'God Consciousness and remaking the world.' I am designing this idea so that it will be financially independent.

I PLAN TO LEAVE THIS EARTH A LITTLE BETTER THAN I FOUND IT.

Donations may be sent to:

AAG Foundation, Inc.
100 Stockton Street
Box 175
Chelsea, MA 02150
Email: tgcmoss@aagfoundation.com

Thank you for taking the time to read this. Feel open to send me your comments. I will try to respond as quickly as possible.

14188597R10107

Made in the USA
Charleston, SC
26 August 2012